CARIBOO GUR SIKH TEMPLE SOCIETY (1979)
P.O. BOX 4038, QUESNEL, B.C.
CANADA V2J 3J2

THE SIKH ☬ CANADIANS

By Manmohan Singh (Moni) Minhas

Reidmore Books Inc.
Edmonton, Alberta, Canada

printed and bound in Canada

© 1994 Reidmore Books

All rights reserved. No part of this work covered by the copyrights hereon may be reproduced or used in any form or by any means—graphic, electronic, or mechanical—without the prior written permission of the publisher. Any request for photocopying, recording, taping, or information storage and retrieval systems of any part of this book shall be directed in writing to CANCOPY, 214 King Street West, Suite 312, Toronto, Ontario M5H 3S6.

Reidmore Books wishes to thank the following people for their insights and support in the development of this book:

- Gian Singh Sandhu of Williams Lake, B.C., World Sikh Organization
- Manjit Singh of Montreal, Quebec, Macauliffe Institute of Sikh Studies
- Dr. Hugh Johnson of Vancouver, B.C., Simon Fraser University

We have made every effort to correctly identify and credit the sources of all photographs, illustrations, and information used in this textbook. Reidmore Books appreciates any further information or corrections; acknowledgment will be given in subsequent editions.

Design & Layout by Pacific Edge Publishing Ltd.

Canadian Cataloguing in Publication Data

Minhas, Manmohan Singh (Moni), 1954–
The Sikh Canadians

    Includes bibliographical references
    ISBN 1-895073-44-8

    1. Sikhs—Canada. 2. Sikhism. 3. Canada—Emigration and immigration. I. Title.
FC106.S55M56 1993   305.6′946071   C93-091903-3
F1035.S54M55 1993

Reidmore Books Inc.
1200 Energy Square
10109 – 106 Street
Edmonton, Alberta   T5J 3L7

Photo Credits

Entries are by page number, coded as follows:
T = Top   B = Bottom   L = Left   R = Right

Front Cover: TL–Westfile/Bill McKeown
                  TR, B–Courtesy M.S. Minhas
Back Cover: L–National Capital Commission
                  R–Westfile/Bill McKeown
vii Westfile/Bill McKeown
  4 Whyte Museum of the Canadian Rockies/V484/NG5–46
  5 T–Vancouver Public Library, B–Courtesy, M.S. Parhar
  8 Courtesy, M.S. Minhas
10 T–British Columbia Archive and Record Service/HP67501
      B–Vancouver Public Library/5236
13 City of Vancouver Archives/CH N.111 P84
16 Vancouver Public Library/6231
17 Vancouver Public Library/6229
19 Courtesy, J.S. Seroya
20 National Archives of Canada/PA 125114
21 Courtesy, S.K. Hari
22 Courtesy, S. Gill
23 Courtesy, G.S. Chowdhury
26 Courtesy, M.S. Minhas
33 Courtesy, M.S. Minhas
35 T–Courtesy, S.S. Mander, B–Prem Photography
37 Courtesy, H.K. Bajwa
40 Imperial War Museum/Q2061
41 Courtesy, T.S. Panchhi
44 Courtesy, M.S. Minhas
45 Courtesy, M.S. Minhas
46 Courtesy, M.S. Minhas
47 Courtesy, M.S. Minhas
49 Courtesy, M.S. Minhas
50 Courtesy, H.N.S. Khalsa
52 Courtesy, J.S. Khalsa
53 Courtesy, J.S. Khalsa
55 Courtesy, B.S. Shergill
56 T–Courtesy, B.S. Shergill, B–Courtesy, M.S. Minhas
57 Courtesy, S.S. Mander
58 Courtesy, M.S. Minhas
60 Courtesy, S.S. Mander
61 T–Courtesy, P. Chohan, B–Courtesy, M.S. Minhas
63 Courtesy, M.S. Minhas
65 Courtesy, S. Sander
67 T–Courtesy, M.S. Minhas, B–Courtesy, H. Doman
68 Courtesy, S.S. Marwah
69 Courtesy, G.S. Sandhu
70 T–Courtesy, D. Sidoo, B–Courtesy, R. Bawa
71 Courtesy, G.S. Hans
72 T–Courtesy, M.S. Sihota, B–Courtesy, G.S. Malhi
73 Courtesy, W.T. Oppal
74 T–Courtesy, Guru R.K. Khalsa, B–Courtesy, M. Deol
75 Courtesy, Hardev Singh
76 Courtesy, S. Dhaliwal

Dedicated to my parents Gurcharan Singh and Gurdev Kaur,
my wife Rani Kaur, and our children Manjit Kaur and Ravinder Singh.

Contents

A Message from the Author   viii

Introduction / Who Are the Sikhs?   1
   Immigration to Canada   3
      The First Sikh Immigrants   4
      Sikhs in Canada Today   7

Chapter 1 / Sikh Migration—An Adventurous People   9
   Immigration between 1903 and 1908   9
   Immigration between 1908 and 1947   12
   Immigration between 1947 and 1966   13
   Immigration from 1967 to Today   14
      The *Komagata Maru* Incident   16
   Profiles of Sikh Pioneers from Each Region of Canada   18
      Sikhs on the West Coast   18
      Sikhs on the Prairies   20
      Sikhs in Central Canada   22
      Sikhs in the Maritimes   23
   Time Line of Sikh Immigration to Canada   24

Chapter 2 / Sikh Religion and History   25
   Sikhism—The Religion   25
      The Development of Sikhism: The Ten Sikh Gurus   26
      The *Khalsa*—"The Brotherhood of True Disciples"   30
      Teachings of Sikhism   31
      The Five Ks of Sikhism   32
      The Symbol of Sikhism—The *Khanda*   33
      Guru Granth Sahib—The Holy Scripture   34
      The *Gurdwara*   35
      Meditation   37
      Sonia Kaur and Navdeep Singh Bajwa (*Gurbani* — "the word of the Guru")   37
   Important Dates in Sikh History   38
   The History of Panjab   39

Chapter 3 / Sikh Culture and Traditions   43

    Traditional Clothes   43
        How to Tie a Turban   46
    Food   47
    Sikh Names   48
    Sikh Religious Ceremonies   49
        Naming   49
        Initiation   49
        Sikhs of Western Origin   50
        Marriage   51
        Death   54
    Family Values and the Role of Women   54
    Dancing and Music   55
    Festivals   57
    The Sikh Calendar   59
    Traditional Sport   59
    Education   61
    Sikh Organizations and the Sikh Press   63

Chapter 4 / Sikhs in Canada Today   65

    Charity   65
    Entrepreneurs   66
    Lumber Industry   67
    Banking   68
    Transportation   68
    Farming   69
    Sports   70
    Politics   72
    Professionals   73
    Entertainment   74
    Art and Literature   75

Conclusion   77

Glossary   78

Sikh *Gurdwaras* in Canada   81

Sikh Calendar   85

Suggested Reading List   86

About the Author

Manmohan Singh (Moni) Minhas was born and raised in India, moving to Canada at the age of 22. He graduated from the University of Calgary with a degree in engineering, and has been working in the petroleum industry for 15 years.

In 1991, he founded his own company, *Minhas Training and Development Inc*, mainly teaching seminars in the U.S.A., Canada, Singapore, Thailand, Indonesia, Malaysia, Russia, Cuba and other countries.

This book is the culmination of several years of research and has been written with the hope of increasing understanding of the heritage, culture and religion of the Sikh Canadians.

A Message from the Author

Sikhs are one of the many ethnic groups that make up the Canadian cultural mosaic. This book explores the story of Sikh Canadians. The Introduction is about who the Sikhs are and why they came to Canada. In Chapter One the reader will be able to trace the pattern of Sikh immigration and read about early Sikh immigrants who settled in various parts of Canada. Chapter Two is a summary of the religion and history of the Sikhs. The culture and traditions of the Sikhs will be discussed in Chapter Three. In the last chapter, Chapter Four, you will read about some present-day Sikh Canadians and their contributions to Canada.

Brief biographies, photographs, maps, and illustrations have been included in this book. The glossary explains some of the Panjabi words and phrases found in the book. These are identified in italics when they appear in the text.

The uniqueness of the Sikh culture and religion is discussed throughout this book, and while both are important and interesting subjects, all humans have largely the same aspirations, joys, and worries. Like most people, Sikhs are trying to make a good living, raise their families, and have at least a little bit of fun along the way! Getting to know a Sikh (or any human being) invariably results in the discovery of the commonality that binds us all.

I hope the readers of this book enjoy the experience of getting to know their Sikh Canadian neighbours. I also encourage you to visit a *Gurdwara*, attend a Sikh wedding, or take part in some other cultural function. People from all religions and cultural backgrounds will be most welcome at all of these places and events.

—Manmohan Singh (Moni) Minhas, 1994

Introduction

WHO ARE THE SIKHS?

*There are no foes nor strangers
For we are all fellow beings.*
—Guru Arjun Dev, the Fifth Guru

Sikhs are those people who believe in the teachings of Sikh Gurus, try to live according to these teachings and beliefs, and perform their rites and ceremonies in accordance with Sikh religion and culture. As with other people, there is a large variation in individual adherence. The Sikh religion originated in Panjab in the northern part of the Indian subcontinent. The word *sikh* means "disciple" or one engaged in learning the higher truths of life. When India became independent in 1947, the country was divided into two countries along religious lines—India and Pakistan. Panjab was also divided between the two countries. After partition, almost all Sikhs and Hindus who lived in the northwest portion of the Panjab were forced to move to the Indian side. Many Muslims living on the Indian side moved to Pakistan. Sikhs are a small minority in comparison with other world religions. They make up less than two per cent of the total population of India. They have a slim majority in their home province of Panjab.

The word *panjab* means "the land of five rivers." Panjab is a beautiful land of snow-fed rivers, high mountains, and fertile valleys. Panjab is called the breadbasket of India, because it produces a significant portion of India's agricultural food products. Agriculture and the hard work of the Panjabis have made Panjab the wealthiest province of India.

Who Are the Sikhs?

Map of India showing Panjab.

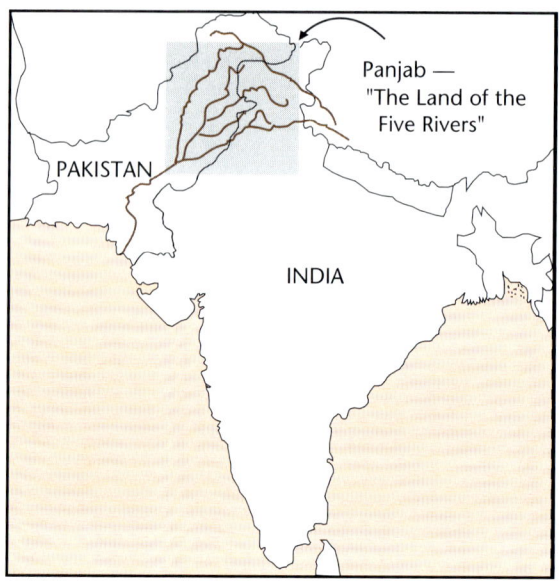

For over a century, Sikhs have shown a willingness to immigrate to different parts of the world and have always quickly adapted to their new surroundings. Almost every country in the world has at least a small Sikh community. Below is an approximate population breakdown of Sikh communities around the world.

Sikh Communities Around the World.

Country	Total Population (Millions)	Sikh Population (Thousands)	(% of total)
Panjab, India	21	11 500	54.76%
Rest of India	875	4 000	0.46%
UK	57	400	0.70%
Canada	27	240	0.89%
USA	274	175	0.06%
Malaysia	17	50	0.29%
Kenya	25	50	0.20%
Singapore	3	15	0.50%
Rest of the world	3700	70	0.001%
Total	**5000**	**16 500**	**0.33%**

There are Sikh communities in Hong Kong, Norway, Switzerland, Japan, Philippines, Indonesia, Iran, Thailand, Australia, Germany, Holland, New Zealand, Uganda, Kuwait, and United Arab Emirates.

Immigration to Canada

There have been Sikhs in Canada for nearly a century. Until 1960, their favourite destination was the west coast of Canada, mainly because of its access to the Pacific Ocean from East Asia. In the last thirty years, Sikhs have settled in other parts of Canada. Today, Vancouver and Toronto have the largest Sikh populations.

Most of the Sikhs who have come to Canada have come from India. Others came from different parts of the world such as Hong Kong, The United Kingdom, Kenya, Tanzania, Uganda, Malaysia, and Singapore. The map below shows the distribution of Sikhs in the different provinces of Canada.

Sikhs made up more than 85 per cent of all East Indians migrating to Canada from 1900 to 1950. This is remarkable since they constitute less than two per cent of the population of India. Their home state of Panjab in India is landlocked, and it has the highest per capita income in India. So why did so many Sikhs come to Canada? The primary reason for their migration to Canada (or to other foreign lands) has been that they are adventurers and have not been afraid to take risks. Also, like most immigrants, they were rich enough to leave their homeland and yet were poor enough to have the motivation to seek opportunities in far-away lands.

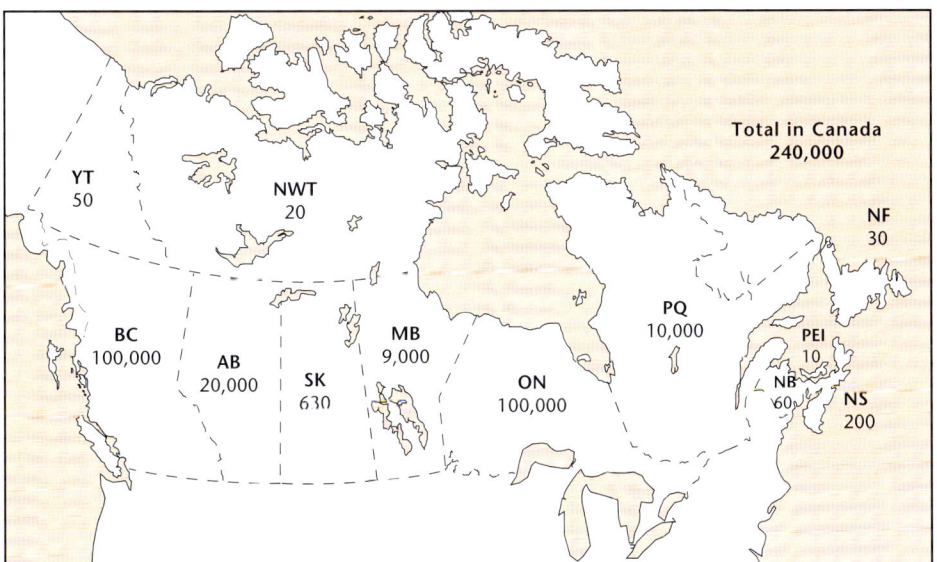

Distribution of Sikhs in Canada.

Who Are the Sikhs?

The First Sikh Immigrants

Sikhs started arriving on a regular basis in 1903. After arrival in Canada, most of them worked in farming, logging, railways, or sawmills. Many eventually started their own fuel delivery, farms, and lumber businesses. Their efforts have helped develop British Columbia's lumber industry.

Sikh bodyguards of the Duke of Cornwall and York (later King George V) during his visit to Banff, Alberta, 1901.

The Journey of Malkit Singh Parhar

Malkit Singh Parhar was three when he came to Canada in 1927 with his mother and his brother. They were going to join his father, who had been in Canada since 1906. It took them two months to reach Canada. First they traveled by train for three days from Panjab to Calcutta, a distance of 1500 kilometres. They stayed in a *Gurdwara* in Calcutta for a week and then boarded a boat to Hong Kong. This boat stopped at several ports en route to Hong Kong, including Colombo (Sri Lanka), Penang (Malaysia), Singapore, and Saigon (Vietnam). They arrived in Hong Kong after sixteen days and stayed in the local *Gurdwara* for twelve days before boarding another ship bound for Canada. This ship stopped at Shanghai (China), Nagasaki (Japan), Kobe (Japan), and Yokohama (Japan). After eighteen days at sea, they arrived in Victoria where they were greeted by Malkit's father.

Who Are the Sikhs?

Sikhs landing in Vancouver, 1904. It was common for Sikh immigrants to be wrongly identified as "Hindus."

During the sea voyage, the Parhars traveled in "steerage class." This means they did not have a cabin. Instead, they lived on the open deck and they had to cook their own food. It was a long and tiring journey. With little to do, some of the passengers used the time to make friends with one another. They even managed to learn the fundamentals of new languages such as Chinese or English from other passengers. This became very helpful since most of the Sikhs on board did not speak English. By the time they reached Canada, a few were able to understand a bit of English.

Malkit Singh Parhar, his father, and mother in Vancouver after their journey.

Who Are the Sikhs?

Cover of Malkit's passport.

Inside pages of Malkit's passport.

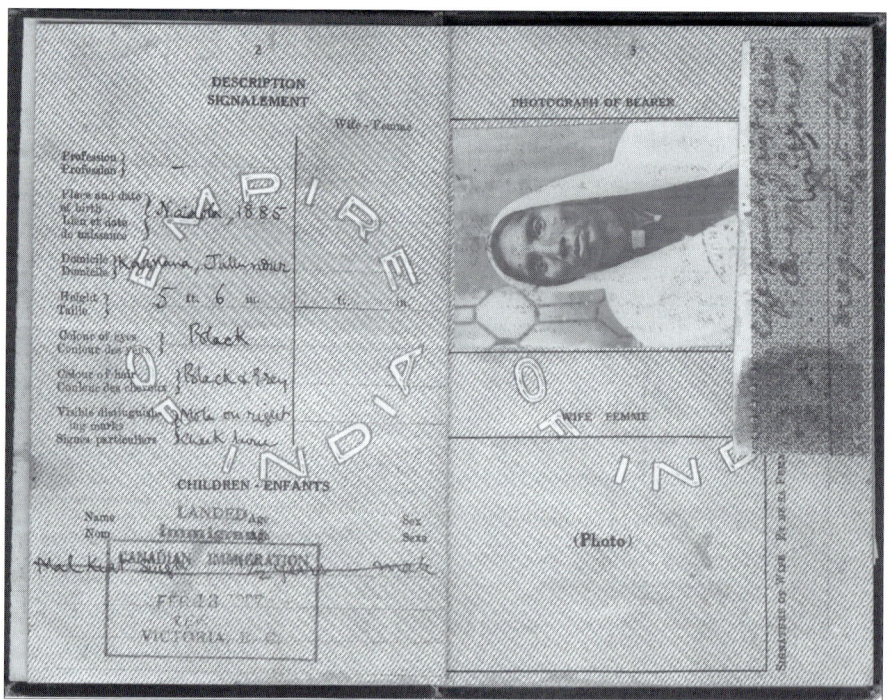

Malkit Singh Parhar's journey to Canada is typical of the way Sikhs traveled to Canada between 1903 and 1950. The entire trip required many stops and connections between India and Canada. During these stops Sikhs stayed at the local *Gurdwara* where they could get free accommodation and meals. It took almost two months to reach their destination. The entire trip cost less than $150 in 1927, but the average Canadian wage then was 30¢ an hour.

Malkit now lives in Vancouver, and his family is spread throughout various parts of Canada and the United States.

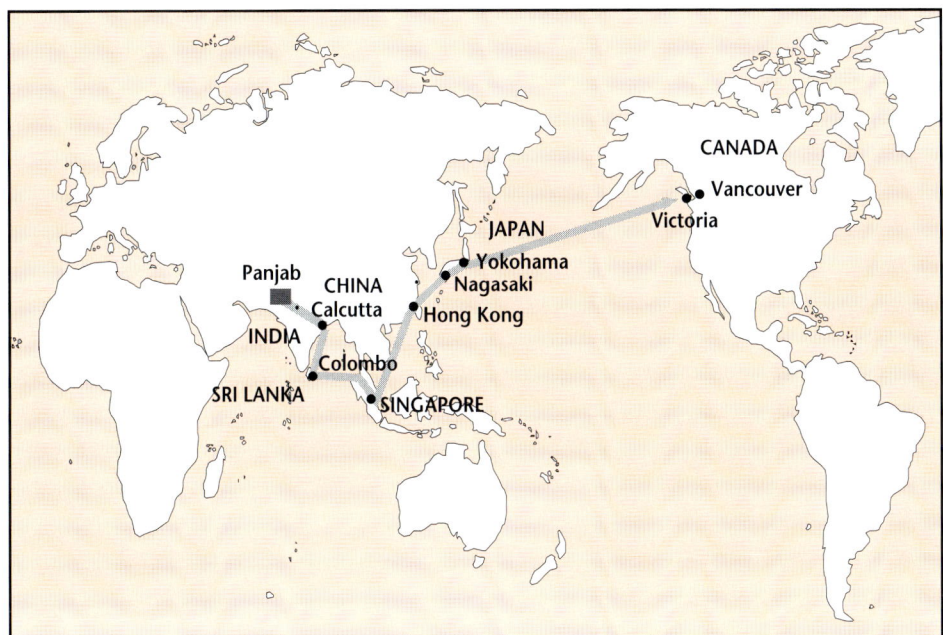

This map shows the route taken by Malkit Singh Parhar when he came to Canada.

Sikhs in Canada Today

The origins of native Canadians go back to prehistoric times. Ancestors of non-native Canadians have migrated from various parts of the world over the last 400 years. These immigrants, together with Canada's aboriginal peoples, have made significant contributions to the nation's multiculturalism.

Most countries have experienced the effects of immigration. When immigrants become assimilated into their new countries they also tend to change the nature of the host countries. This is the case in Canada where immigration has gone on for many years.

Who Are the Sikhs?

Sikhs have been immigrating to Canada for almost a century. As evidenced by their steady rate of migration, Sikhs consider Canada to be a good place to live and raise their families. Sikh experience in Canada has been generally good, although they have faced some very tough challenges.

Because of restrictions in currency export from India, a vast majority of Sikhs came to Canada with only a few dollars in their pockets. Thanks to their attitude and work ethic, and to the opportunities available in Canada, Sikhs have adapted very well to their new economic, social and political surroundings.

Today, over 240 000 Sikhs participate in every facet of Canadian life. Sikh communities of around 100 000 thrive in Vancouver and Toronto. Edmonton, Calgary, Winnipeg, and Montreal are each home to some 7000 to 9000 Sikhs.

A Sikh man walking on a Calgary street during the Stampede.

Chapter One

SIKH MIGRATION— AN ADVENTUROUS PEOPLE

*Recognize all the
human race as one.*
—Guru Gobind Singh, the Tenth Guru

Immigration between 1903 and 1908

Like most other immigrants, Sikhs came to this country to better themselves economically. Frequent changes in Canadian laws over the years caused the number of immigrants from all countries to rise and fall, including that of Sikhs. It should, however, be noted that Sikh immigration compared to migration from many other countries has always been very small.

The first significant immigration of Sikhs to Canada occurred between 1903 and 1908. A British Indian regiment based in Hong Kong, consisting mostly of Sikh soldiers, traveled in 1902 to England by way of Canada to the coronation of Edward VII. Soon after this experience, some of these soldiers led the first significant Sikh immigration to Canada, drawn to its beauty and opportunities for work. The lush Canadian prairies fascinated these men, many of whom came from farming families. The British Indian regiment was disbanded shortly after their return to Hong Kong. It was also at this time that their homeland, Panjab, was going through some hard times due to famine. Soon, many of the regiment's Sikh members began to immigrate to Canada. Many of these men planned to work for a few years and then return to India after they had saved some money. By 1908, about 5000 Sikh men had come to Canada, most of whom settled in British Columbia.

The Sikh men traveled in groups. Their journeys were similar to that of Malkit Singh Parhar, described earlier.

Sikh Migration—An Adventurous People

Sikhs at work in sawmills in the Queen Charlotte Islands.

Sikh men in Vancouver in 1904.

Sikh Migration—An Adventurous People

Young Sikhs on a farm in British Columbia, late 1920s.

When they arrived in Canada, only a few spoke English. The first to arrive organized to help those who came after them. Friends, relatives, and volunteers from the local Sikh community helped them get settled and look for jobs. Most of the early Sikh immigrants eventually found work on farms, in logging camps, on railways, or at sawmills in British Columbia.

Immigration between 1908 and 1947

Sikhs had a long history of military service in British armies and believed that they had equal rights within the British Empire. However, this belief was not shared by the Government of Canada or by many of the citizens of British Columbia. By 1907, public opinion and the trade unions in British Columbia had become strongly opposed to Sikh and other immigration from India. The newspapers were also running a campaign against these immigrants. The Government of Canada wanted to stop their immigration, but was concerned that such a move might generate resentment against British rule in India.

In 1908, the Government of Canada issued an order-in-council requiring that any immigrant arriving at a Canadian port must have come on a continuous journey from his or her country of origin. In other words, they had to come on a direct ship from their country of origin or have purchased a ticket for through fare from her or his home port all the way to Canada. As no shipping line operated between India and Canada and no through ticket could be purchased between these countries, a "continuous journey" from India to Canada was impossible.

Another order-in-council was approved in 1908 requiring all immigrants to bring at least $200 with them to Canada. This also presented a major obstacle to the Sikhs because their wages in India were only about $50 per year. These discriminatory barriers were challenged by the Sikhs in the Canadian court system. They had some moderate victories; however, successive Canadian governments modified the legislation and kept the immigration from India to a minimum.

These new rules reduced Sikh immigration from 2700 in 1907 to an average of only 20 per year over the next forty years. Ironically, while Sikhs were being severely discriminated against, the Canadian West was being settled. Benefits of migrating to the West were being aggressively marketed and hundreds of thousands of immigrant families from Europe and the United States moved to Canada. At the same time, Sikhs already in Canada could not bring their families; Sikhs even had difficulty reentering Canada. All these changes and restrictions caused them severe isolation from their families in India. Many Sikhs decided to move to the west coast of the United States.

While these years were a painful time for the Sikhs in Canada, it was also a period of growth and development, and laid the foundation for today's Sikh communities in Canada. In 1907, Sikhs formed a religious, social, and political organization, the Khalsa Diwan Society. It became the voice of all Sikhs and non-Sikhs from India for many decades. *Gurdwaras* were built in Vancouver, Victoria, and other cities in British Columbia.

Khalsa Diwan Society's Gurdwara in Vancouver. Built in 1908, it was the first in Canada.

After twenty years of lobbying, the Canadian government changed immigration legislation in 1919 to allow Sikh immigrants to reenter Canada freely. They could also bring their families with them. Many Sikhs returned to India and brought their families back with them to Canada. Despite these changes, very few new Sikhs were allowed to migrate to Canada. Over the next thirty years, the second generation of Sikh Canadians was born and raised. Several became successful entrepreneurs. Many moved from British Columbia to various parts of Canada, especially to Ontario, Quebec, Alberta, and other western provinces. Sikh soldiers also served for Canada in the two world wars.

Immigration between 1947 and 1966

When the Sikhs first came to B.C., they were not allowed to vote or to work as professionals. After years of lobbying by the community, Sikhs were finally given the right to vote in 1947 and to join various professions.

Most of the Sikhs who came to Canada before 1947 planned to work for a few years and then return to India after they had saved some money. However, by the early 1950s, Sikhs were no longer as eager to return to India. Similar to the experience of other immigrant groups, they had changed their way of thinking. Many of these Sikhs had grown up in Canada. Unlike the earliest immigrants, they knew this country much better than India. To many of them, Canada was their permanent and only homeland.

In 1951, an annual quota of 150 immigrants from India was approved by the federal government. This quota was increased to 300 immigrants in 1957. These measures increased the Sikh immigration moderately. In addition, several Sikh professionals migrated to Canada during this period.

In 1967, the Canadian government introduced the point system for approving immigration. The government used this system to determine whether or not a person qualified for immigration. When a person applied for immigration, the government would consider his or her age, education, professional and language skills, and so forth. The applicant was given points in each of these categories. The younger and better educated received more points. English and/or French language skills were also important. If a person were sponsored by a Canadian resident or had prearranged employment and a minimum of fifty points, he or she was allowed to immigrate.

Many of the Sikhs who came to Canada under the point system in the 1960s settled in the Prairies, Ontario, and the Maritimes.

Immigration from 1967 to Today

In 1967 many more Sikhs came to Canada when the Canadian government began accepting applications for immigration from people who were visiting the country. In 1973, the number of Sikh immigrants rose dramatically when the Canadian government decided to grant landed immigrant status to thousands of Sikhs who had applied for immigration while visiting Canada. From 1972 to 1975, many Sikhs also immigrated to Canada from East Africa—Kenya, Tanzania, and Uganda—and the United Kingdom

Most of the Sikh immigrants who came in the 1960s were skilled workers or entrepreneurs. This is especially true for those who came under the point system. They settled down all across Canada, and formed large communities in Vancouver, Calgary, Edmonton, Winnipeg, and Toronto. Sikh immigration has continued steadily since then.

Today, most Sikh immigrants to Canada fall under two categories, those who come to be reunited with their families and those who come with cash to invest in businesses. In the former category, an applicant for immigration must be a member of the immediate family of a Canadian citizen. This includes spouses, children, or parents. In the latter category, these entrepreneurs are expected to generate employment for Canadian citizens or residents.

Sikh Migration—An Adventurous People

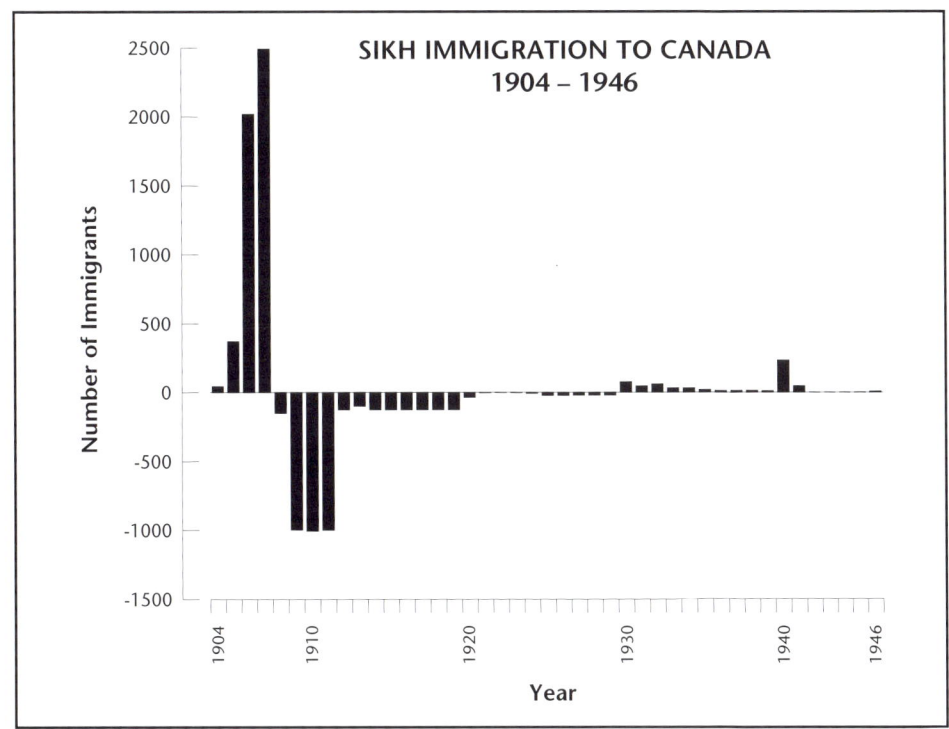

These graphs show the number of Sikhs who migrated to Canada between 1904 and 1990.

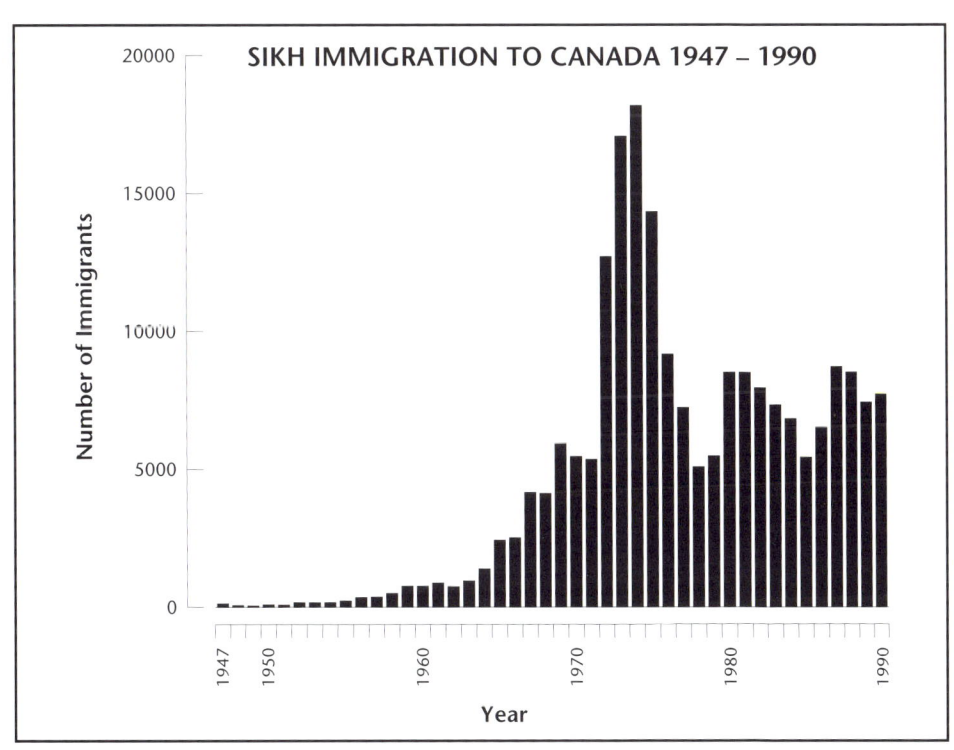

Sikh Migration—An Adventurous People

The Komagata Maru Incident

In 1914, a Sikh, Gurdit Singh Sarhali, decided to bring immigrants from India to Canada by ship. He advertised his plans in several major Asian cities. With a large down payment, he chartered the *Komagata Maru*, an old freighter, from a Japanese shipping company. This ship set sail from Hong Kong on April 6, 1914. It picked up a total of 376 passengers along the way. A large majority of them were Sikhs.

Gurdit Singh Sarhali (first on left, front row) on board the Komagata Maru.

The ship anchored at Burrard Inlet in Vancouver on May 23, 1914, but only twenty-two of the passengers who had previously been in Canada were allowed to land. The rest were asked to go back.

Negotiations began between the Canadian government and the passengers. To help the passengers, the Khalsa Diwan Society's *Gurdwara* in Vancouver set up a support committee consisting of Bhag Singh, Balwant Singh, Mit Singh and Husain Rahim—all members of the Ghadr party, which was fighting for Indian independence. They raised money to help pay for food, legal fees, and the money owed to the shipping company. The government was represented by Malcolm Reid, an immigration officer, William Hopkinson, a government officer and coordinator of a spy ring within the East Indian community, H. H. Stevens, an MP, and Robie Reid, a lawyer. The passengers were represented by the shore committee and their lawyer, Edward Bird.

As negotiations continued, the living conditions on board were getting poor. Food and water were scarce. The support committee made protests but the government did not allow passengers to land in Canada. The ship remained at anchor in the waters off Vancouver.

The Canadian government planned to go through deportation proceedings for one person and apply the same ruling to all the others. The Sikhs were opposed to this proposal because they felt each passenger should have his own hearing. Supplies of food and water were used as negotiating tools by the Canadian government officials. With the worsening situation on the ship, Sikhs reluctantly agreed to the government's plan. The passengers elected a young farmer, Munshi Singh, to represent them for the crucial case. His testimony that he was a farmer and not an artisan or labourer was not believed. Immigration rules at the time did not allow artisans and labourers into British Columbia. As a result, the Board of Enquiry ruled that the *Komagata Maru* passengers would not be allowed to land.

After several days of negotiations, the passengers were given food and medical supplies. The next day, on July 23, 1914, the *Komagata Maru* sailed back to the Far East with thousands cheering on the Vancouver docks. World War I broke out while the ship was returning to Asia.

The Komagata Maru *leaving Vancouver, with* HMS Rainbow *in the foreground.*

Their ordeal was not over. Passengers of the *Komagata Maru* were not allowed to land in Hong Kong or Singapore, their points of origin for the arduous journey. The British Indian government shipped all the Sikhs to India. When the ship docked near Calcutta, the government wanted them to board a train and go directly to Panjab. The passengers feared that the British would imprison them. They left the ship and walked away from the waiting train. Panic and confusion occurred and the police started shooting. Twenty-six people were killed and thirty-five were seriously wounded. The bitterness caused by this series of incidents also caused violence between the Sikhs who supported the *Komagata Maru* passengers on one hand, and Canadian government informers within the Sikh community and the Canadian government officials on the other hand. This resulted in the murders of William Hopkinson and four Sikhs, and the hanging of Mewa Singh, priest of the Khalsa Diwan Society *Gurdwara*.

In May 1993, the Government of Canada issued an apology to the Sikhs for the *Komagata Maru* incident. Ironically, Gurdit Singh Sarhali's great granddaughter has also recently migrated to Toronto, Ontario.

Profiles of Sikh Pioneers from Each Region of Canada

Sikhs on the West Coast

Up until 1960, most Sikhs preferred to settle on the West Coast. Immigrants from Asia landed in Vancouver because it was the closest port of entry. It was natural for these immigrants to settle around the area where they first set foot.

Mayo Singh and Bishan Kaur Manhas

Mayo Singh Manhas came to Canada in 1906. He worked at sawmills and on railways. Eventually, he started a sawmill business with some of his friends and relatives.

After operating two sawmills on Vancouver's lower mainland, Mayo and his partners bought a sawmill and 400 acres of timber rights near Duncan, B.C., in 1917. They named the place Paldi after Mayo's village in Panjab. Over the next fifty years they were very successful in their business ventures and expanded significantly. They also built a school, a Sikh *Gurdwara*, and a Japanese temple. They expanded their lumber rights to more than 14 000 acres

(5665 hectares) in various parts of British Columbia. Mayo became the first Sikh industrialist in Canada.

When Mayo was thirty-seven, he returned to India to get married. His marriage had been arranged by his parents. Soon after, his wife, Bishan Kaur, moved to Canada.

Mayo Singh and Bishan Kaur Manhas.

Mayo and his wife Bishan Kaur were very generous and charitable. Mayo's generosity led the media in British Columbia to call him "Santa Claus All Year Round." Mayo and Bishan made contributions to hospitals in British Columbia by supplying fruits, vegetables, and linens for several years. They also provided free room and board to new immigrants at Paldi until they found work. The University of Victoria has recently set up a scholarship in Mayo's name.

Some members of Mayo's family are still living in Paldi today. The *Gurdwara* which he built continues to serve the Sikhs of Duncan, British Columbia.

Sikh Migration—An Adventurous People

Sikhs on the Prairies

Most of the Sikh immigrants who came to Canada in the 1960s obtained their landed status under the point system. Many of them were professionals. It was also at this time that there was a shortage of school teachers and doctors in the Prairies. Many Sikh immigrants saw this as an opportunity to pursue their chosen careers. They began coming to the Prairies to find work and settle down.

Some of the earliest Sikh immigrants to the Prairies at Frank, Alberta railway station in 1903.

Sikh Migration—An Adventurous People

Sujan Kaur Hari

"Harnam Singh Hari, my father-in-law, came to Canada in 1908. He worked in a sawmill in Vancouver for two years and then moved to Calgary. He worked very hard, and eventually became a large landowner. He owned more than 5000 acres (2023 hectares) of land in south Calgary and area. My husband, Ujagar Singh Hari, came to Calgary in 1925. He visited India a few years later and while there we got married through family connections.

"I came to Canada with my husband in 1929. We traveled by boat from Calcutta. We had to stop over in Hong Kong for two and a half months, and during that time, we stayed at the local *Gurdwara*.

Sujan Kaur Hari with her great granddaughter, Vanessa.

"My marriage was arranged by my parents. It was very exciting coming to a new country and starting a new family. I was fascinated by a lot of things, especially Western clothes. My husband and I took part in a lot of social and cultural activities. We lived on a farm in Alberta and we raised nine children. We kept alive the traditions of the Sikhs. Like other immigrants, our family has adapted very well to Canadian life. Our children are all grown up now, and many have married non-Sikhs."

Sikhs in Central Canada

Sikhs began coming to central Canada on a regular basis in the 1950s, attracted by the manufacturing industry of southern Ontario. Today, most of the Sikh immigrants coming to Canada settle in or around the Toronto area.

The Gill Brothers of Toronto

Two of the first Sikhs to settle in central Canada were the Gill brothers. Jimmyat (Jimmy) Singh Gill came to Vancouver, B.C., in 1928 at the age of eighteen. His uncle, who was one of the passengers on the *Komagata Maru*, had encouraged him to come to Canada.

The Gill Brothers, Maghar (left), and Jimmyat.

Jimmy moved to Toronto in the early 1930s. Soon after, his younger brother, Maghar (Major) Singh, came to join him. The two brothers began a business partnership in 1946 when they opened the India Trading Company. The company imported engraved handicrafts, food items, and fabrics from around the world, and sold them through wholesale and retail outlets. In 1963, they opened India House, the first Indian restaurant in Toronto. Both businesses lasted for twenty-five years.

Jimmy and Major returned to India and married two sisters and soon they returned with them to Toronto. The two families lived in the same house until their last days. They were deeply religious and were instrumental in the building of the first Sikh *Gurdwara* in Toronto. As well, they helped many Sikh immigrants settle in Canada.

Sikhs in the Maritimes

As early as 1909, some Sikhs entered Canada through Halifax, Nova Scotia, perhaps because they felt that there would be a more favourable reception there than in the West. However, they usually moved to Toronto or Vancouver. Two of the first Sikh immigrants to make a permanent home in the Maritimes were Gajinder Singh Chowdhury and Rupa Kaur Chowdhury.

Gajinder Singh and Rupa Kaur Chowdhury

Gajinder Singh Chowdhury was twenty-six when he came to Halifax in 1959. He attended Dalhousie University and studied education. After graduation, he taught in Halifax. In 1963, he returned to India for a marriage arranged by his parents and those of his wife-to-be, Rupa. Rupa moved to Halifax with Gajinder, attended Dalhousie University, and also became a teacher. Both Gajinder and Rupa are now retired and living in Halifax. The Chowdhuries were founding members of the Sikh *Gurdwara* in Halifax that was built in 1975.

Gajinder and Rupa Chowdhury in Halifax, 1963.

Sikh Migration—An Adventurous People

Time Line of Sikh Immigration to Canada

1902 A British Indian regiment based in Hong Kong, consisting mostly of Sikh soldiers, traveled to England by way of Canada to the coronation of Edward VII. Some of these soldiers led the first significant Sikh immigration soon after this experience, drawn to Canada's beauty and opportunities for work. Most settled in British Columbia.

1907 All "natives of India not of Anglo-Saxon parents" were disenfranchised by the British Columbia provincial government. For the next forty years, they could not vote in civic, provincial, or federal elections, join the public service or certain professions.

1908 The first *Gurdwara* in Canada was built by the Khalsa Diwan Society in Vancouver. The first Sikh in Canada also took *Amrit* (Sikh initiation) and got married.

1908 The continuous journey legislation was passed by the federal government, bringing Sikh immigration to a standstill because it required that immigrants travel to Canada without any stopovers, an impossibility for Sikhs.

1912 The first Sikh Canadian, Hardial Singh Atwal, was born in Vancouver.

1914 The *Komagata Maru* incident took place. After two months in Vancouver harbour, the 376 Southern Asian passengers on board were refused entry into Canada and were forced to return to Asia.

1919 A change in the legislation allowed families of Sikh residents to enter Canada. Many Sikhs returned to India for their families.

1947 The continuous journey legislation was repealed. Sikhs and other people from India were given the vote and allowed to work as professionals in British Columbia.

1951 An annual quota for 150 immigrants to come to Canada from India was approved by the federal government.

1957 The annual quota of immigration to Canada from India increased to 300.

1960s Many Sikh school teachers and professionals immigrated to the Prairies, Ontario, and the Maritimes. Sikh communities sprang up across Canada.

1967 The Point System for approving immigration applications was introduced. It replaced the quota system. The second major Sikh immigration started when the Canadian government began accepting applications for immigration from people who were visiting Canada.

1973 The Canadian government granted landed immigrant status to those visitors who remained in the country. Several Sikhs and immigrants from other countries benefited from this. Many Sikhs also immigrated to Canada from East Africa and the United Kingdom under these rules.

1973 Steady Sikh immigration started and has continued to date.

Chapter Two

SIKH RELIGION AND HISTORY

*Be not estranged from another
for God dwells in every heart.*
—Sri Guru Granth Sahib

The Sikhs' religion is called Sikhism. In this chapter, you will look at some of the teachings of Sikhism and how they affect the way Sikhs live. In addition, because it is important to know that the history of the Sikhs had a direct influence on the teachings of Sikhism, you will read about Sikh history.

As with followers of other religions, Sikhs sometimes have more than one interpretation of their religion's teachings and history. Also like other people, not all Sikhs choose to follow all the teachings of Sikhism. In this chapter, the most commonly accepted Sikh history and teachings are presented.

Sikhism—The Religion

Sikhism first arose through the teachings of Nanak Dev, the First Guru, in Panjab in the sixteenth century. The main principles of Sikhism are one God, service to fellow human beings, sharing one's earnings with the needy, equality for women, equality for all, and acceptance of all religions. Sikhism was developed by the teachings of ten successive *gurus*, named by their predecessors, over a period of more than 230 years. It is believed that the soul of Guru Nanak was transferred to each succeeding Guru. All ten gurus referred to themselves as "Nanak" and there is complete consistency in their teachings.

Over two centuries, Sikhs faced many obstacles to their faith. The rulers of India at that time were the Moguls who persecuted non-Muslims for their beliefs. Faced with these conditions, Sikhs became strong defenders of Sikhism and other religions.

The Development of Sikhism: The Ten Sikh Gurus

Selfless service to humans brings us nearer to God.
—Guru Nanak Dev, the First Guru

A detailed description of the development of Sikhism is beyond the scope of this book. A brief summary of each of the ten Gurus is given below as an introduction to the development of Sikh religion.

Beginnings—The Birth of Sikhism (1469 to 1539)

I. Guru Nanak Dev (born 1469, died 1539)

The First Guru, Nanak Dev, was born in 1469 in northern India. Even as a child Nanak enjoyed being with holy men and taking part in religious discussions. By the time he was fifteen, he had studied both Hinduism and Islam in depth. He had also learned many languages, such as Sanskrit, Persian, and Arabic.

Child holding picture of Guru Nanak Dev - the First Guru.

When he was thirty, Nanak had a profound religious experience, a vision of God. One day, while he was bathing in a river, he vanished. Three days later he emerged, a changed man, claiming that he had seen God and proclaiming, "I am neither a Hindu nor a Muslim. All are equal before the one God."

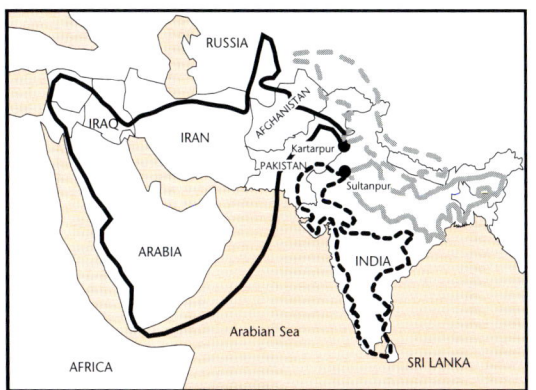

Guru Nanak's Travels

From then on, Guru Nanak began to preach the universality of humankind, abolition of the caste system, equality, and meditation on God's name. He went on preaching tours, and in twenty years, he had traveled over a very large area of India, Persia, and the Middle East. His preachings emphasized what people shared, not what set them apart. Guru Nanak preached in Panjabi, the language of the common people, so more people of Panjab could understand his teachings. He established community kitchens (*langars*) to emphasize service to fellow human beings, removal of the caste system, and equality among humans. He taught that, as all are equal, salvation is available to all through living a moral and responsible family life as well as through devotion to God.

"The Root Hymn" by Guru Nanak, the First Guru, gives the essence of God.

Expansion of Sikhism (1539-1606)

II. Guru Angad Dev (born 1504, Guru 1539 to 1552)
Chosen for his humility and discipleship, Angad Dev compiled the hymns and teachings of Guru Nanak in written form. To do this, he refined and finalized the Panjabi alphabet which became *Gurmukhi* script, the language of the Sikh holy scriptures, and thereby gave Sikhs their own written language. He opened more *langars* and was well known for his generosity, wisdom, and love of children. He also started a tradition of physical fitness among Sikhs.

III. Guru Amar Das (born 1479, Guru 1552 to 1574)
Amar Das spread the teachings of Gurus Nanak and Angad and developed specifically Sikh ceremonies and rites for birth, marriage, and death. He furthered the equality of women by fighting against *purdah* ("isolation of women") and *sati* ("burning of widows on their husbands' pyres"). He also encouraged widows to remarry.

IV. Guru Ram Das (born 1534, Guru 1574 to 1581)
Ram Das promoted missionary activities, set up a central treasury and founded the Sacred Sarovar ("Lake of Immortality") around which his successor would build Amritsar ("pool of nectar"), the Sikh holy city.

V. Guru Arjun Dev (born 1563, Guru 1581 to 1606)
Arjun Dev organized the building of the Golden Temple, Harimandir, in Amritsar. As a sign of respect for all religions, he asked a Muslim Sufi, Mian Mir, to lay the foundations of the holy temple. He contributed a large volume of hymns to the Sikh holy scriptures and compiled the *Granth Sahib*, the Sikh scriptures. Arjun Dev was martyred in 1606 by the Emperor Jehangir, who accused Arjun of treason.

Religion in Revolt (1606 to 1644)

VI. Guru Hargobind (born 1595, Guru 1606 to 1644)
Hargobind became Guru at the age of eleven after the death of his father Arjun. He wore two swords, representing the need for spiritual and secular responsibility, an important Sikh tenet. He introduced a pennant which became the Sikh flag, "the Nishan Sahib." He built Akal Takht, across from the Golden Temple in Amritsar, a centre to guide the Sikhs in temporal matters. It also served as Sikhism's supreme court. It grew into an institution which symbolizes the idea that the use of the sword for the protection of righteousness and for self-defense is not wrong. He reinforced the concept of the saint-soldier in Sikhism.

Peaceful Consolidation (1644 to 1664)

VII. Guru Har Rai (born 1630, Guru 1644 to 1661)
Har Rai was endowed with a peace-loving nature and a reflective mind. He emphasized free kitchens and organized many religious congregations and started a new organization to preach Sikhism in various parts of the land. He also taught the Sikhs to help others, even if they had been unkind in the past, when he saved the life of the son of Mogul Emperor Shah Jehan.

VIII. Guru Hari Krishen (born 1656, Guru 1661 to 1664)
Hari Krishen became Guru at the age of five. Though he only lived to the age of eight, he served as an example to young children, teaching by example to obey and to act on the advice of one's parents. He served and healed thousands of people who were poor and suffering from cholera.

IX. Guru Tegh Bahadur (born 1621, Guru 1664 to 1675)
Tegh Bahadur preached forgiveness as a virtue. He was martyred in 1675 for protecting Hindus from religious persecution by the Mogul Emperor Aurangzeb. Tegh Bahadur believed that all human beings, including Hindus, should be allowed to practise their own religion.

Culmination (1675 to 1708)

X. Guru Gobind Singh (born 1666, Guru 1675 to 1708)
A scholar, a poet, and a warrior, Gobind Singh combined the qualities of his most illustrious predecessors. He wrote a great many hymns, later collected in the *Dasam Granth,* or "Book of the Tenth Guru." He created the *Khalsa*, "the brotherhood of true disciples," and the Five Ks of Sikhism. The Tenth Guru expanded and edited the *Granth Sahib*. He decided there would be no human guru after him, and before his death, he transferred his spiritual authority to the *Granth Sahib*. The holy book became known thereafter as the *Guru Granth Sahib*.

The Khalsa—"The Brotherhood of True Disciples"

Every religion, through history and tradition, has an event which comes to represent the ultimate spiritual experience for its followers. For Muslims, it is fasting during the month of Ramadan. For Christians, it is the crucifixion and the resurrection of Christ. For Buddhists, it is the time when Prince Siddhartha experienced nirvana (enlightenment) after deep meditations under the *bodhi* tree. And for the Sikhs, it was the creation of the order of *Khalsa*, the brotherhood of true disciples in 1699.

Guru Gobind Singh, the tenth and last human guru, invited all Sikhs to attend the festival of *Baisakhi* at the village of Anandpur, Panjab. When the people were gathered together, the Guru spoke of the difficult time facing them and the need for courage and sacrifice. Then, he brandished his sword and asked, "Is there one here who will give his head for the truth?" Many in the congregation left. After repeated calls, one Sikh offered himself. The Guru took the disciple into a nearby tent, a thud of steel meeting flesh and bone was heard, and a stream of blood began to flow from beneath the tent.

The Guru emerged with his sword dripping blood. He called for another martyr. Again many left. Finally another disciple came forward. They went into the tent and the same horrifying sound of steel hitting flesh was heard and a stream of blood flowed from under the tent. Guru Gobind repeated this until five martyrs had come forward.

The last time, there was a longer pause in the tent. Finally, the Guru came out with all five disciples, alive and well, wearing clothes dyed with saffron. All wore turbans on their heads and swords at their sides.

The five Sikhs were initiated (*amrit*) the next day. They became the *Panj Pyares* ("five beloved ones") and they were renamed *Singh* ("lion"). A code of conduct for the Sikhs was also established including the Five Ks. (The Five Ks are discussed in detail later in this chapter.)

Then, the Guru requested the *Panj Pyares* to admit him to the order of the *Khalsa*. In imposing the same regimen on himself, the Guru made a powerful statement of standards that were to govern the Sikhs and reinforced Sikhism's democratic traditions. The Guru also told them to baptize all Sikhs similarly. He asked the men to take the name *Singh* and the women to take the name *Kaur* ("princess").

Teachings of Sikhism

Sikhism strives to guide people in their daily lives. The basic teaching of Sikhism is for humankind to exist affably and on equal terms. Some of the basic principles of Sikhism are:

1. One God who has no shape or form—Sikhs believe there is only one God, the Creator of this universe.

2. Equality for all humankind—Sikhs believe that everyone is equal, regardless of their ethnic, racial, or religious origin and beliefs.

3. Equality for women—Sikhs believe that women and men should have equal rights and privileges.

4. The Three Fundamental Rules of Sikhism are:
   Nam Japo—meditation on God's name
   Kirt Karo—dignity through honest and hard work
   Wand Chako—sharing one's earnings with the needy

5. Acceptance of all religions—Sikhism is not opposed to other faiths. The Gurus never claimed Sikhism as the only way to God and salvation.

6. A strong family life—Sikhism asks its followers to lead the life of a householder and a family person.

7. Sikhism prohibits smoking, alcohol, and the use of intoxicating drugs, adultery, cutting of one's hair, eating meat in the *Gurdwaras*, and superstitious and ritual practices. There is no special injunction against beef or pork.

Khalsas vow to follow the teachings of Sikhism closely and to observe the Khalsa code of conduct. This includes the five symbols which Sikhs wear as reminders to fulfill their religious obligations. These symbols are very important to a Sikh. They identify, remind, and teach the Sikhs to do honourable deeds in their lives. The five symbols are known as the Five Ks of Sikhism because they all begin with the letter "K."

The Five Ks of Sikhism

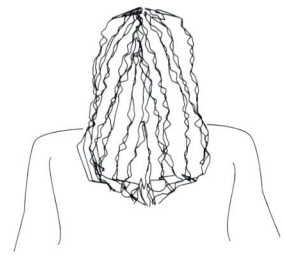

1. *Kes* ("uncut hair"): As you have read in the previous section, one of the prohibitions of Sikhism is cutting one's hair. Sikh men wear their long hair in a knot on the top of the head. A *dastar* ("turban") is worn to cover it. *Kes* represents a simple life, saintliness, wisdom, and devotion to God.

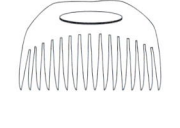

2. *Kanga* ("wooden comb"): The *kanga* is worn to keep the hair tidy. It represents a clean mind and body. The mind should be free of impure thoughts.

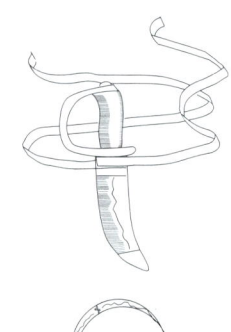

3. *Kirpan* ("sword"): The *kirpan* is worn at the waist. It represents freedom and indomitable spirit, and calls for the Sikhs to stand up for the oppressed.

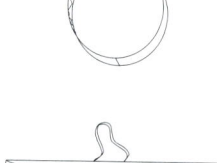

4. *Kara* ("steel bracelet"): The *kara* is worn on the wrist and is a sign of the eternity of God who has no beginning or end. It is also a reminder not to misuse the hands.

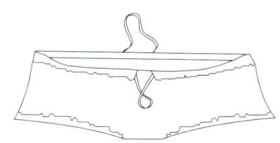

5. *Kacha* ("short breeches"): Sikhs wear the *kacha* as a reminder to observe chastity, modesty, and sexual restraint.

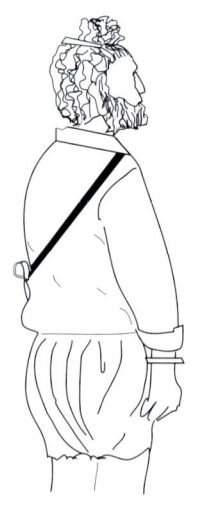

Those Sikhs who choose to follow all of the above teachings of Sikhism or observe all the Five Ks are called *Amritdharis*, or *Khalsa*. The term *Kesadharis* ("ones with long hair") refers to Sikhs who do not cut their hair, do wear a turban, but may or may not keep the other Ks. They are not *Khalsa*, and have not taken the initiation ceremony. *Sahajdharis* ("slow adapters") observe only some of the teachings and requirements. They are called slow adapters because they are thought of by some of the *Khalsa* as Sikhs who will be joining the order of the *Khalsa* at a future date.

The Symbol of Sikhism—The Khanda

Like most religions, Sikhism also has a symbol. It is called a *Khanda*. It represents the basic teachings. It is made up of three parts, and each part has its own special meaning that is symbolic of the beliefs and obligations of a Sikh.

The two swords on the outside represent the need for both spiritual and worldly responsibilities, for a balance between a person's need for spiritual salvation and his or her worldly obligation to society. The circle stands for God who is perfect and eternal, without beginning or end. In the middle is the khanda ("double-edged sword"). It represents divine knowledge. The two sharp edges divide truth from falsehood.

The Sikh Flag — Nishan Sahib

The Sikh flag (Nishan Sahib) is triangular in shape with the Khanda, the Sikh symbol, in the middle. The flag is made from a saffron-coloured cloth and is mounted on a highly constructed platform, representing the irrevocable spirit of the Sikhs.

Two Nishan Sahibs are placed before all *Gurdwaras* to represent the spiritual and temporal responsibilities of Sikhs. Every Baisakhi, the Nishan Sahib is ceremoniously changed after the requisite prayers. It is also ceremoniously carried by the Five Beloved Panj Pyares ahead of the Guru Granth Sahib, in any Sikh procession.

Guru Granth Sahib—The Holy Scripture

We have read how the Tenth Guru decided there would be no more Gurus in human form after him and that he instructed the Sikhs to regard the *Guru Granth Sahib* (the Holy Scripture) as their teacher and guide. From then on, Sikhs have regarded the holy scripture with the same respect they showed their human gurus.

The *Guru Granth Sahib* contains 1430 pages of hymns and verses and has thirty-three sections. The first section contains the masterpiece composition "*Japji*" by Guru Nanak which beautifully sums up the essence of the *Guru Granth Sahib*. The last section is a collection of assorted verses. The remaining thirty-one sections contain hymns, with each section named after Indian classical music pieces (called ragas). Some of these ragas were also created by the Gurus themselves.

Guru Granth Sahib is a unique holy scripture in the following ways:

- A new alphabet (*Gurmukhi*) was composed for it by the Second Guru, Guru Angad Dev.
- Its contents were recorded by the Gurus themselves, not by their followers.
- It contains compositions by thirty-seven individuals including seven Sikh Gurus and thirty other saints whose message was in perfect harmony with the teachings of the Gurus. These thirty individuals were from various religions (Hindus and Muslims), castes (high and low), and social status (rich and poor).
- It is treated with great reverence, the same as was given to the human Gurus.

The book is kept in a worshipping room and is treated with great respect. On entering this room, one must cover one's head and remove one's shoes. The *Guru Granth Sahib* reveals the teachings of Sikhism, directs Sikhs in their daily lives, and promotes the message of love and harmony among all humans. Most Sikh religious ceremonies are performed in the presence of the holy book.

While the *Guru Granth Sahib* is being read, it is placed on a special platform and covered by a canopy. When not in use, it is kept wrapped and surrounded with embroidered clothes and cushions.

The Gurdwara

Sikh Gurdwara *in Vancouver, designed by Arthur Erikson.*

A *Gurdwara* is a place of worship for the Sikhs. The first *Gurdwara* in Canada was built eighty-six years ago. At present, there are more than eighty *Gurdwaras* across Canada. *Gurdwaras* typically have a prayer hall, a *langar*, classrooms, a library, and an office.

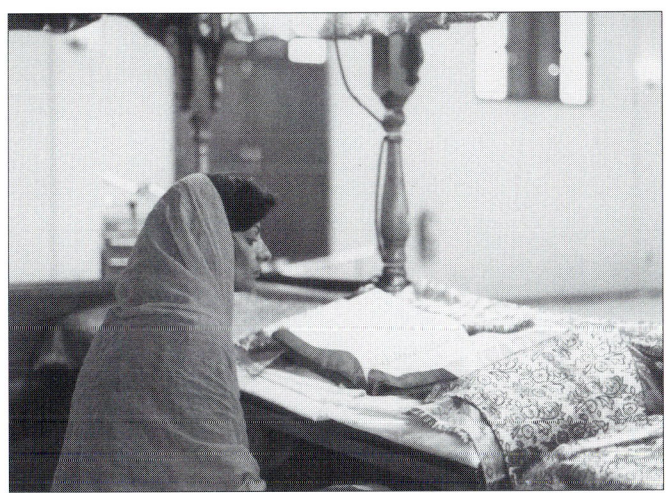

A Sikh woman reading the Guru Granth Sahib.

Religious services are held daily, early in the morning. The congregation sits on the carpeted floor. During the service there is reading and singing of hymns and verses from the *Guru Granth Sahib*, meditation, and religious dissertations. People may come and leave at any time during the service.

Before the service ends, a member of the congregation randomly opens the *Guru Granth Sahib* and reads the first verse on the left page. This is called *Hukam Nama* (directive for the day or occasion). Finally, *karah parsad,* made of flour, water, sugar, and clarified butter, is distributed.

*Gurdwara*s are not only places of worship, they are also the training centres for hospitality and service to fellow human beings. This role has always formed an integral part of the *Gurdwaras* around the world. In fact, a *Gurdwara* without *Guru Ka Langar* is incomplete and inconceivable. "Bread and water belong to the Lord—and the desire to serve, the pleasure of the Sikhs" is the common utterance of Guru's disciples when serving in the free kitchen.

After the service in the main prayer hall is finished, the congregation then goes to the *langar* to share a meal together. The food is free, and families take turns preparing it. In the *langar*, everyone sits in rows and eats together to emphasize equality for all.

The *Gurdwara* is run by a committee of volunteers elected by the congregation. Many Sikhs have a worshipping room in their own homes kept especially for housing the *Guru Granth Sahib,* daily prayers, and meditation.

Everyone, including non-Sikhs, is welcome to attend Sikh religious services. The only requirements are the removal of shoes and covering of heads before entering the prayer hall. Scarves are available at the door for those who need them. Tobacco, alcohol, intoxicating drugs, and meat are strictly prohibited in *Gurdwaras.*

Besides serving as a place of worship, *Gurdwaras* are also social meeting places for the Sikh communities. *Gurdwaras* in Canada organize many educational, cultural, charitable, and traditional events for the local communities. Through the *Gurdwaras,* Sikhs donate large sums of money and goods to various charitable organizations, hospitals, and disaster relief agencies across Canada and around the world. Schools in *Gurdwaras* offer classes to youth and adults in Panjabi and English. They also hold Sikh youth camps, sporting events, and special functions for seniors. *Gurdwaras* usually contain a library which has books and audio and video tapes dealing with Sikh religion, culture, and history. These materials are primarily in English and Panjabi; some are in Urdu, Hindi, and French.

Gurdwaras around the world offer free accommodation to those who need it. You don't have to be a Sikh to enjoy this. This is a Sikh tradition. It is something that has been in existence since the founding of the Sikh religion. As in other religions, community service and service to humankind are very important parts of Sikhism. The *Gurdwara* is operated by the Sikhs in this spirit and tradition.

Meditation

One of the tenets of Sikhism is meditation on God's name. Many Sikhs meditate daily. There is no restriction on the time spent on meditation. A beginner usually meditates for a few minutes. After a while, she or he can do it for a longer time. Sikhs meditate to discipline their minds and purify their souls, but it is also a good way to relax.

Meditating is fairly simple and easy. All you need is a little practice and concentration. Here is what to do:

1. Find a quiet place where you can sit comfortably.

2. Choose a word that has no associated meanings for you to recite. Sikhs usually recite *Satnam Waheguru,* which means "Almighty God's name is truth."

3. Close your eyes and repeat the word you have chosen over and over.

4. Concentrate on reciting the word and try not to think about anything else. It may not be easy at first, but keep trying and soon it will become easier.

Sonia Kaur and Navdeep Singh Bajwa

Gurbani, "the word of the Guru," is of paramount importance in the Sikh religion. Children, youth, and old people alike participate in the songs, teaching, and study of the *Gurbani.* Sonia Kaur and Navdeep Singh Bajwa are fine examples of this long-standing tradition. This sister and brother team have been trained in playing classical Indian musical instruments and regularly perform in *Shabad Kirtan* (singing hymns) in local *Gurdwaras* in the Toronto area. They have won many awards and have placed first in competitions. Sonia and Navdeep placed first in their age group in the regional finals of the Sri Hemkunt Foundation Symposium held in Buffalo, New York, in April 1993. Both practise their music for at least one hour every day and are top students academically.

Important Dates in Sikh History

1469–1708 Sikhism was founded and developed by the Ten Gurus.

1708–1716 Political consolidation period of Banda Singh Bahadur (1670-1716).

1748 Creation of the *Dal Khalsa,* the Sikh army, which was divided into twelve militias, or *misls*.

1799–1839 The rule of Maharaja Ranjit Singh (b. 1780). Called the "Lion of the Panjab," Ranjit Singh united the Panjab, removed the threat of invasion, and built a strong, prosperous kingdom. He respected other faiths (his court had Muslims, Hindus, and Sikhs). His death brought the Panjab back into chaos and, within the next ten years, the British were able to defeat the Sikh Kingdom and annex the Panjab.

1849 Britain annexed Panjab and placed the ten-year-old Maharaja Dileep Singh, Ranjit Singh's son, under house arrest.

1857 The Indian Sepoy Mutiny. The beginning of a sixty-year period of cordial relations between the British and the Sikhs.

1861–1891 The British developed the Canal Colonies in northern Panjab. Sikh farmers began moving to this area. The Singh Sabha Movement, which was very successful in rekindling the Sikh spirit and consciousness, was also started.

1895 Sikh immigration to various countries began.

1914–1919 World War I. Sikhs made up twenty per cent of the British Indian Army and had an outstanding record for heroism.

1919 Jallianwala Bagh Massacre in Amritsar, Panjab, took place. Large numbers of Sikhs joined the Indian Independence Movement. Sikh contribution to the movement was immense.

1925 The British passed the Gurdwaras Act, giving the Shiromani Gurdwara Parbhandhak Committee (SGPC), a body elected through the universal suffrage of Sikh voters, control of more than two hundred historical Gurdwaras.

1947 India gained independence. The country was partitioned into Pakistan and India.

1966 Panjab was further divided, giving Sikhs a slim majority in their home province of Panjab.

1984 After months of disputes, the Government of India ordered an attack on Sikh separatists in the Golden Temple in Amritsar. Prime Minister of India, Indira Gandhi, was assassinated a few months later by two Sikh bodyguards seeking revenge. This was immediately followed by angry mobs of people killing thousands of innocent Sikhs in major cities across India.

The History of Panjab

A few years after the death of the Tenth Guru, Guru Gobind Singh, one of his disciples, Banda Singh Bahadur, formed a very effective *Khalsa* army. By 1715, he and his army took over a large area of northern India. Then in 1716, fate turned against Banda. His small army was overwhelmed by various rulers in the area. Banda and his army were surrounded and starved into surrender.

The Sikh armies kept a low profile for the next forty years. Various invaders were coming from the north and destroying the centuries-old Mogul Empire. Sikh armies usually stayed out of the way of the invaders when they went through Panjab on the way to Delhi. They were content in attacking the intruders as they returned home, freeing their captives and running away with their loot.

By the late 1760s, remarkable Sikh leaders such as Nawab Kapur Singh, Jassa Singh Ahluwalia, and Jassa Singh Ramgarhia began to emerge. The military reputation of the *Khalsa* was slowly rebuilding. At the same time, the Mogul Empire was falling apart after ruling India for more than two hundred years. Aware of their small population base, Sikh leaders had earlier started a unique military organization by dividing Panjab into twelve *misls* ("militias"). Every Sikh was free to join any *misl* he chose. All were considered equals. They combined freedom of individual action with the discipline of a unified command.

The organization of *misls* effectively channeled the energies of the fiercely independent *Khalsa* soldiers. The *misls* acted together in the interests of the community and protected each other. The *misl* system lasted several decades. For the first time in history, they defeated the Afghan, Mogul, and other invaders from the north. The tradition among northern Indian Hindu families of raising their first son as a Sikh also started during this time. This tradition lasted over one hundred and fifty years. By the late eighteenth century, control of the *misls* became hereditary. The organization lost its leadership and the *misl* system started to become fractious and disjointed.

In the 1790s, one of the Sikh military leaders, Ranjit Singh, united the *misls* and formed a united Sikh kingdom. He became the *maharaja* ("great king") of Panjab. He ruled Panjab for forty years until his death in 1839. In 1849, the British took control of Panjab, the last major part of the Indian subcontinent to fall under British rule.

After 1849, thousands of Sikhs were recruited into the British Indian Army. Panjab went through a period of sustained development. New roads, railways, post offices, and telegraph facilities were developed. In 1857, the Indian Sepoy Mutiny took place. A group of Hindu and Muslim Indian soldiers in the British Indian Army rebelled against the British when the men found out that new rifle cartridges had been greased with beef and pork fat, the eating of which was prohibited by their respective religions. Before using the cartridges, it was necessary to bite into them which meant that the men would have to come into direct contact with animal fats offensive to their religious beliefs. Some British were killed in the mutiny, but many of the Sikhs stood by the British and defended them. This was the beginning of a sixty-year period of good relations between the British and the Sikhs.

From 1861 to 1891, the British developed northern Panjab by building irrigation canals. The area was called the Canal Colonies, and many Sikh farmers were encouraged to move to this area. The condition of the farmlands had been greatly improved and Sikhs who moved there gained significant benefits from these developments.

Sikhs serving the British Indian Army in World War I.

At the same time, British Indian regiments were sent to different parts of India and to other British colonies in Asia such as Hong Kong, Shanghai, Malaysia, and Singapore. Sikh immigration to different parts of the world, including Canada, began from these colonies. Contact with the outside world made Sikhs realize the lack of political rights they had in their own country. The discontent made the overseas Sikhs, especially those from the west coasts of Canada and the United States, form the Ghadr Party with the goal of achieving independence for India. Their counterparts in India were not in a position to challenge the enormous British power. After initial success, the movement was effectively suppressed.

During World War I, twenty per cent of the British Indian forces were Sikhs. They were noted for their bravery, winning fourteen out of the twenty-two military crosses awarded for gallantry.

The cordial relations between the Sikhs and the British began to decline after the Jallianwala Bagh Massacre in Amritsar. On April 13, 1919, a division of the British Indian Army attacked a meeting on Indian independence. The army opened fire at the Sikhs, Hindus, and Muslims without warning, killing 379 and injuring over 2000. After the massacre, many Sikhs and other East Indians joined the Indian Independence Movement in large numbers. Sikhs participated very actively in the struggle for Indian Independence.

India gained its independence from Britain in 1947, but the country was partitioned on religious grounds into two countries, Pakistan and India. Sixty-two per cent of the original Panjab lands were given to Pakistan. At the time of partition, some Sikhs demanded their own country. However, they were not successful because they were a minority and lacked unanimous support among themselves. The separatist movement which began at that time has continued to this day.

The partitioning of India resulted in outbreaks of communal violence and the sudden immigration of more than ten million people. More than two million Sikhs moved to the Indian side of the border. About forty per cent of Sikhs became homeless and many were killed during this period. In 1966, Panjab was further divided and Sikhs were left with a slim majority in their home province.

The Golden Temple at Amritsar.

In spite of the initial period of upheaval after independence, Sikhs have prospered throughout India, actively participating in the political, social, and economic life there. Notwithstanding the above, some Sikhs in India have for several decades been demanding a separate independent nation, to be called Khalistan, based on the premise that the distinct culture and religion of the Sikhs were being discriminated against and even persecuted. After years of simmering political disputes, violence broke out and some Sikh separatists led by Sant Jarnail Singh Bhindranwale occupied the building next to the Golden Temple. In 1984, the Government of India ordered the army to flush out the separatists from the building. The attack lasted for four days. Over one thousand people were killed or wounded, including the separatist leader and worshippers who were in the Golden Temple at the time. The shrine itself was seriously damaged. In revenge, Prime Minister Indira Gandhi was assassinated by two of her Sikh bodyguards a few months later. In response to her death, angry mobs began looting Sikh property and killing thousands of innocent Sikhs in major cities across India.

The attack on the Golden Temple by the Indian Army and other incidents have captured the attention and support of many Sikhs for the separatist movement and they continue to press for the creation of Khalistan.

Maharaja Ranjit Singh

In 1792, at the age of twelve, Ranjit Singh inherited a large territory in central Panjab from his father, Maha Singh, who was one of the strongest leaders in the warring confederacy of *misls*. When Ranjit Singh was seventeen years old, he took control of these territories and expanded them. Ranjit Singh liquidated all the warring *misls* of Panjab. At nineteen, he captured Lahore and made it his capital.

Ranjit Singh was a progressive-thinking, enlightened, and fair ruler. His dream was to build a Panjabi kingdom. He did not allow indiscriminate destruction of life or property. During his rule, he never passed a death sentence. He modernized and expanded his army, an army of men from all religions. He hired military advisors from Europe who brought the concept of military drills and marches to teach discipline among the ranks of soldiers. With his well-trained army, Ranjit Singh was the first leader to defeat the Afghan invaders from the north of India.

Ranjit Singh rebuilt and enlarged the Golden Temple in Amritsar. The British, who had ruled most of India for more than a hundred years, wanted Panjab for themselves. However, the British and Ranjit Singh respected each other's powers and they signed a treaty of friendship in 1809.

When Ranjit Singh died in 1839 at the age of fifty-nine, fighting broke out between his army and family. In 1849, after two Sikh-British wars, the British annexed Panjab. Ranjit Singh's ten-year-old son, Dileep Singh, was placed under house arrest. The British promised to return the Sikh kingdom to the rightful heir as soon as he was old enough to take on the responsibility but they reneged on the promise and the kingdom was never returned.

Chapter Three

SIKH CULTURE AND TRADITIONS

*When all other means of ending injustice
have been exhausted, it is only
just to wield the sword.*
—Guru Gobind Singh, the Tenth Guru

Sikh culture and tradition is a part of northern Indian culture, where Panjab is. Sikhs in Canada combine both traditional and Western culture in their lives.

Traditional Clothes

Sikhs in Canada wear Panjabi as well as Western clothes. Most of the older Sikhs in Canada wear Panjabi clothes because they find them to be more comfortable. The younger Sikhs wear Western clothes most of the time, a sign of their acceptance of Western society. These younger Sikhs often wear Panjabi clothes when they go to *Gurdwaras* or when they attend Sikh ceremonies.

The traditional apparel for Sikh women is the *salwaar-kameez*, also called a Panjabi suit. Sikh women in Canada usually wear the *salwaar-kameez* when they go to the *Gurdwaras* and parties, and it is traditionally worn with a lot of jewels and accessories. For example, around the ankles, some women wear a silver bracelet called the *jhanjran*. The spot you see on the foreheads of Sikh women is called the *bindi*. A decoration called *paranda* is braided into the hair. It helps to make the hair look longer. Sikh women usually wear embroidered shoes with the *salwaar-kameez*.

Sikh woman in traditional clothes.

The traditional clothes worn by Sikh men consist of a *tamba, kurta shirt*, and *achkan*. The *tamba* is a sash worn around the waist with a *kurta*-style shirt. When the weather is cold, they wear the *achkan* on top as a coat. Some Sikhs wear the *kurta* pajama. In Canada where the winters are cold, Sikhs wear parkas and heavy coats just like anybody else.

Sikh man in traditional clothes.

The *dastar*, or turban, has a very deep religious and cultural meaning for the Sikhs. As described in Chapter 2, all male Sikhs with long hair are required to wear a *dastar*, or turban, that is wound around the head to cover the hair. A *dastar* is a long piece of cloth, usually five metres long by one metre wide. The colour and style of a turban have no religious meaning. Some Sikhs choose to wear a particular coloured turban all the time (like red or blue); it becomes their trademark. Most match the colour of their turban with the rest of the clothes they are wearing. Most older Sikhs wear lighter coloured turbans, including white. The style and colour of the turban can sometimes be indicative of the geographical origin or country of the person wearing it. Tying a turban does not come naturally and can be a bit awkward because of the length of the cloth. One has to practise and learn the art of tying a turban. Young Sikhs often ask their fathers to help them until they can do it on their own.

The turban, over the centuries, has also come to represent pride and respect to the Sikhs. Exchanging turbans between two people makes them *Guru Bhai* or "brothers by the grace of the Guru." Their families and descendants would continue to have intimate relationships for generations to come, based on this brotherly relationship. Similarly, the ultimate act of humility and remorse is to lay one's turban on the other person's feet. Touching or knocking a Sikh's turban is very disrespectful.

Male Sikhs wear a headcovering called a *patka* when they are young. They start wearing turbans only when they have reached adolescence. Women, like men, are also required to keep their heads covered. Usually, they cover their heads with a *chunni* but a few also wear a *dastar*.

> *Keep the God given form intact with a turban donned on your head.*
> —Guru Arjun Dev, the Fifth Guru

Sikh boy in patka. (left)

Sikh boy in turban. (right)

Sikh Culture and Traditions

How to Tie a Turban

Food

Sikhs are famous for their hearty appetites. The traditional Sikh staple is *roti* which is an unleavened bread made from whole wheat flour. It is often served with curries, barbecued meats, rice, vegetables, and lentils.

One of the favourite Sikh snacks is *pakoras*. They are delicious and quite easy to make. Below is a recipe for making *pakoras*. You may want to try it out. The ingredients are available from your regular grocery store.

Pakoras

180 ml (3/4 cup) chick pea (*besan*) flour
10 ml (2 teaspoons) lemon juice
5 ml (1 teaspoon) salt
5 ml (1 teaspoon) chili powder
3 ml (1/2 teaspoon) ground black pepper
1 onion finely chopped
1 potato finely chopped
125 grams (1/2 cup) of chopped cauliflower
spinach finely chopped
250 ml (1 cup) water
oil for deep frying

Combine the flour, lemon juice, salt, chili powder, black pepper, onion, potato, cauliflower, and spinach in a large bowl. Make a well in the centre. Gradually mix in the water and stir until well blended.

Heat the oil. Spoon batter carefully into hot oil a few spoonfuls at a time and deep fry until golden brown. Remove and drain on absorbent paper. Keep hot. Repeat until all the batter has been fried. Serve hot with ketchup or Indian chutney.

Sikh Names

Sikhs take great pride in their names. Like other Canadians, Sikhs have first names, middle names, and last names. Naming a Sikh child takes place at an important religious ceremony.

Most Sikh first names can be used by girls or boys. In fact, it used to be quite common for a sister and a brother to have the same first names but be identified by their middle names. Sikhs use Singh as a middle name for males and Kaur for females. Sikh Canadians sometimes anglicize their names so other Canadians will find them easier to pronounce.

Many first names are formed by combining two words. For example, Manjeet is a combination of *man*, which means "heart," and *jeet*, which means "winner." So, Manjeet really means "winner of the heart" or "one who has won over (or controlled) their hearts." Another example is Harbir which is made up of *har*, meaning "God," and *bir*, meaning "brave." So Harbir means "brave by the grace of God."

The last names of Sikhs usually come from one of the following four sources:

(a) Singh or Kaur—As described earlier, the Tenth Guru of the Sikhs asked his people to adopt the last name of Singh for males and Kaur for females. Until the mid-1940s, almost all Sikh Canadians adhered to this system. At that time, some started using other last names described below and used Singh and Kaur as their middle names. However, Singh and Kaur are still the most common last names among the Sikhs.

(b) Clans—All Sikhs belong to a clan. Many Sikhs have last names that are the same as their clan names, such as Minhas.

(c) Ancestral villages—Some Sikhs prefer to use the names of their ancestral villages for their last names. Bhindrawale is such a name.

(d) Adopted names—Some Sikhs drop their original last names and adopt a different one. Some adopt Khalsa as their last name because it identifies the person as a Sikh. In the early 1900s, there was a trend among Sikh immigrants in British Columbia to adopt their father's first name as a last name. Examples are Robin Bawa and Herb Doman.

Sikh Religious Ceremonies

Most Sikh religious ceremonies are performed in the *Gurdwara* and in the presence of the *Guru Granth Sahib*. Messages from the Scripture are very important to the Sikhs and, because of that, passages from the *Guru Granth Sahib* are always read as a part of the ceremonies. Because Sikhs believe everyone is equal, any person, male or female, may perform the ceremonies. The four major Sikh ceremonies are the naming of babies, initiation, marriage, and death.

Naming

Naming a child is performed in the *Gurdwara*. After prayers are said, a person randomly opens the *Guru Granth Sahib*. The first letter of the alphabet on the left-hand page will be the first letter of the child's name.

Initiation

In Sikhism, initiation is performed by personal choice. A person can receive initiation only after she or he understands its obligations, usually after adolescence, when one feels emotionally and spiritually ready to take the initiation vows.

During the initiation ceremony, five *Khalsa* men or women are chosen to prepare *amrit* ("nectar of immortality"). The *amrit* is prepared in an iron bowl by stirring the *patasas* (sugar crystals) and water with a *khanda* ("double-edged sword") while saying the requisite prayers. The five *Khalsa* each say one prayer. The person to be initiated bows before the *Guru Granth Sahib* as the initiation vows are being read. Drops of *amrit* are then sprinkled in his or her face, his head and then everyone drinks the *amrit* from the same bowl, as a sign of equality and brotherhood. Once a person is baptized, he or she is admitted to the order of the *Khalsa*. From then on, the person is expected to fulfill the obligations of a Sikh and to follow the *Khalsa* code of conduct.

An Amritdhari Sikh serves food to the needy at a downtown Calgary soup kitchen.

Sikhs of Western Origin

Hari Nam Singh Khalsa

Born in Toronto as David Friedman, Khalsa adopted Sikhism in the 1970s. He is one of many people of Western origin who have chosen the Sikh way of life.

Hari Nam closely follows the Khalsa Code of Conduct, beginning his day at 4 AM with morning prayers, yoga exercises, and meditation. He also spends a lot of his time teaching and working with the youth in Toronto and the rest of Canada.

As he describes, "I find the world very tense and uptight. I can see the pain on the faces of many people I encounter. The Sikh way of life gives me a beautiful sense of well being and elevation."

Marriage

A Sikh marriage is not only a spiritual and physical union of the bride and groom, but it is also a union of the two families. There are three stages in a Sikh marriage— matchmaking, pre-wedding, and wedding.

Matchmaking

As is the custom in most Asian cultures, Sikh marriages have traditionally been arranged by matchmaking, where the parents try to find suitable spouses for their children. They will look for individuals with similar personalities, education, social, and economic backgrounds. Today, many parents no longer arrange marriages for their sons or daughters, but they still try to assist in the matchmaking by introducing their children to prospective spouses. It is then up to the two individuals to decide if they want to be married or not.

Pre-wedding

The second stage of a Sikh marriage is the pre-wedding ceremony. During this ceremony, the groom-to-be sits in front of the *Guru Granth Sahib*. After prayers are said, the relatives of the bride-to-be give him sweets, fruit baskets, dried dates, coconut, and money. In return, the relatives of the groom-to-be give the bride-to-be some sweets, money, henna leaves, and other gifts. On the night before the wedding, there is a ladies *sangeet* or wedding shower held in honour of the bride. At the same time, there is a bachelor party held in honour of the groom. On both occasions, there is plenty of music, dancing, and food.

Wedding

Sikh weddings are held in the *Gurdwara* and are elaborate and delightful events. The parents of the bride and groom make all the necessary arrangements and take care of the expenses. The wedding ceremony can take place on any mutually convenient date. Looking for auspicious days or using horoscopes is contrary to Sikh beliefs. In Canada, weddings are frequently held on a Saturday, in the late morning. The bride and groom can wear anything they like, traditional Panjabi clothes or Western wedding clothes.

On the day of the wedding, the *barat* (groom's wedding party) usually arrives at the bride's house around midmorning. They are greeted by the *raagis* (professional religious singers). After that, the morning prayer is said, followed by the *milni* ceremony and a light breakfast. The *milni* ceremony is a union of the two families. The respective parents, brothers, and sisters from the bride's and the groom's side exchange formal greetings, flower garlands, hugs, and gifts. Everyone then goes to the main hall of the *Gurdwara* for the wedding ceremony.

In the *Gurdwara*, the couple sits in front of the *Guru Granth Sahib*, while the person who performs the wedding speaks of the virtues, obligations, responsibilities, and importance of a marriage. The bride's father then gives the bride away by giving her the *palla*, symbol of union. The *palla* is a piece of long cloth that the groom has carried into the ceremony with him. Right at the moment the *palla* is handed over, the *raagis* start singing this hymn:

> *Praise and blame I both forsake,*
> *I seize the edge of your garment.*
> *All else I let pass.*
> *All relations I find false.*
> *I cling to thee.*

A bride and groom hold the palla.

Sikh Culture and Traditions

The religious part of a Sikh wedding ceremony is called *Anand Karaj* or "Ceremony of Bliss." It consists of a person reading a particular stanza from *Guru Granth Sahib*, followed by a group of people singing the same verse while the couple walks around the *Guru Granth Sahib*. This is done four times as there are four verses to be read and sung. After that, the couple is pronounced husband and wife. The congregation then prays for a happy and successful marriage. The ceremony ends with the distribution of *Karah Parsad* ("sacrament") to everyone.

The bride and groom receive flower garlands and gifts.

Flower garlands are placed around the couple's necks to symbolize blessings from their families. Money is also given to the couple and to charity. When this is over, everyone goes to the *langar* for a meal. In the evening, there is usually a Western-style reception with dancing and a dinner party.

Death

In Sikhism, death is treated as part of the normal life cycle. The bereaved are asked to seek comfort and guidance from the hymns and teachings of the *Guru Granth Sahib* and to accept death as God's will. The building of funeral monuments is not in accordance with Sikh beliefs.

The body is bathed, the Five Ks are left on the body, and then it is cremated. A close relative lights the pyre and the mourners sing appropriate hymns from the *Guru Granth Sahib*. Exhibitions of grief such as screaming or chest-beating are not in accordance with the Sikh teachings. After cremation, an *Akhand Path* is started. This consists of uninterrupted reading of the *Guru Granth Sahib* from cover to cover by a series of people, a forty-eight hour process.

Relatives usually give gifts to the poor and donate money to the *Gurdwara* and charities. The remains of the body are disposed of in any running water such as a stream or a river.

Sikh Gurus preached that the human soul goes through cycles of birth and death. After experiencing life in many forms (such as animals and insects), the soul is born as a human being. If a Sikh follows the teachings of the Guru, the soul is liberated from transmigration.

Death and the funeral ceremony are excellent reminders of human beings' self-centredness and the need to remember God and to follow the Gurus' teachings in everyday life.

Family Values and the Role of Women

As in the lives of many other Canadians, the family plays a central role in the lives of Sikh Canadians. In the case of first- and second-generation immigrants, the family provides cultural continuity when individuals have to adapt quickly to a new economic, social, and cultural system outside the home. The second generation children may also have the additional responsibility of providing translation, banking, and other assistance for the first generation when dealing with the unfamiliar outside world.

Within the family structure, women are the main purveyors of Sikh culture, values, and religion. A vast majority of Sikh Canadian women work outside the home. They have the additional responsibility of raising the children and running the household. This work ethic and their traditional family values mean that Sikh women play a very important role.

Like other immigrants, Sikhs go through joys and tribulations in putting down and growing roots in their adopted country.

Sikh Culture and Traditions

Dancing and Music

The *Bhangra* and *Gidda* are the traditional folk dances of the Sikhs and are very popular among Sikh Canadians. Many Canadian cities have *Bhangra* and *Gidda* dance groups that perform regularly at heritage, multicultural, and sports events.

Sikh Bhangra *dancers*

In recent years, several Panjabi *Bhangra* teams from England have become very popular among Panjabi music lovers around the world. They combine Indian and Western tunes with Panjabi lyrics. Some of these groups go on regular concert tours to major cities in Canada and the United States. Canadian cities also have professional *Bhangra* bands.

Major cities in Canada have radio programs in Panjabi. Dozens of television programs are produced locally as well as nationally. There are even twenty-four hour radio and satellite Panjabi television programs across Canada. *Bhangra* music is now being mixed with rap and reggae, is quickly becoming popular among Sikhs and non-Sikhs, and is being played at mainstream bars and dance halls around the world.

Sikh Culture and Traditions

Sikh Gidda *dancers*

Examples of Canadian Bhangra and Panjabi Music

A strong Panjabi and *Bhangra* music industry is now developing in Canada. Examples of some Canadian audio tapes are given.

Festivals

There are two kinds of Sikh festivals, religious and social. Religious festivals are always celebrated in *Gurdwaras*. In India, these festivals are occasions for national holidays. It is rather difficult for Sikhs in Canada to celebrate festivals that fall on weekdays because of work and school. Therefore, Sikh Canadians celebrate their religious festivals on weekends.

Sikh religious festivals are celebrated in memory of the Gurus, their teachings, and to commemorate the establishment of the *Khalsa*. Sikhs celebrate the birthdays of their martyrs who were killed defending their own and others' faiths. Guru Arjun Dev, the Fifth Guru, was martyred by the Mogul emperor. He was forced to sit in a burning pot and was boiled alive. During his torture, he was denied drinking water. This took place in the month of June which is the hottest month of the year. To commemorate this, on his festival day, Sikhs in India give out free cool drinks to people on the streets as a reminder of the Guru's sufferings.

Guru Tegh Bahadur, the Ninth Guru, was beheaded for protecting the Hindus. He disagreed with the Mogul rulers who wanted to force the Hindus to convert to Islam. Sikhs believe everyone has a right to practise his or her own religion.

Baisakhi is the most important, most joyful, Sikh festival. *Baisakhi* is both a religious and a social festival. On this day, usually April 13, the Sikhs celebrate the founding of the order of the *Khalsa*. They also celebrate the Sikh new year and the end of the spring wheat harvest for farmers in Panjab. For several decades, Sikhs in major cities across Canada have been organizing parades as part of the *Baisakhi* celebrations. Parades in Vancouver and Toronto are very big events which attract large crowds of people every year.

Five Pyares, Baisakhi parade.

Sikh Culture and Traditions

Social Festivals

Sikh Canadians celebrate various social festivals based on where they were born or raised and on their family traditions. Two of the most common festivals celebrated are *Diwali* and *Rakhri*. *Diwali* is a festival of lights and involves exchanging sweets with friends and relatives.

A sister putting a rakhri on her brother's wrist.

Rakhri, held in August or September, is a festival that celebrates the love between a brother and a sister. On this day, the sister puts a *rakhri* ("ribbon") on her brother's wrist and a sweet in his mouth. In return, the brother gives the sister some money. It is not surprising to know that brothers usually complain they are always the ones to give money and not the sisters. They would like to be the ones to receive money for a change!

Many Sikh Canadian families also celebrate, usually in nonreligious ways, Western occasions such as Christmas and Easter. They celebrate other occasions such as Father's Day and Mother's Day the same way as other Canadians. Housewarmings, starting a new business, sending children to school, leaving home permanently or on a trip to a far-away spot, and similar occasions are begun by invoking God's blessing. A prayer or *ardas* is said at all Sikh religious functions. Depending on the occasion and the choice of the individual, this can be preceded with *Shabad Kirtan* (hymns), or *Akhand Path*, a continuous reading of the *Guru Granth Sahib*. In each case *Guru Ka Langar* is also served.

The Sikh Calendar

Sikhs follow the Indian lunar calendar to work out the dates of festivals. Each lunar month is the time between two new moons. The lunar calendar is divided into twelve months and, as the lunar year is shorter than the solar year, an extra month is added every third year.

Sikh festivals fall on a different day of the solar calendar each year. Sikh New Year begins on the first day of *Baisakh*, the second month of the Indian lunar calendar. April 13, 1994 marks the beginning of the year 294 on the Sikh (*Khalsa*) calendar.

The Gurus were great lovers of nature. They described nature's beauty as God's great creation in hymns they wrote, including the *Baramaha Tukhari* by Guru Nanak, which has a special hymn for each month. These hymns are sung on the first of each month. The hymn for the first month, *Chet* (March-April), is given below in its English translation.

> **Chet**
>
> Pretty butterflies welcome spring in Chet
> Plants are blossoming in the meadow
> Black birds singing in the mango tree
> Bees wander from flower to flower,
> New life is springing from the winter dead.
> But in my heart there is pain of thy absence,
> Loved one come home
> Nanak seeks the bliss and equanimity of thy union.

Traditional Sport

Sikhs participate and excel in many sports. Their favourite sports are soccer, cricket, field hockey, *Kabaddi* (a rural sport from Panjab), and track and field. Sikh Canadians take part in soccer, field hockey, ice hockey, and other sports. Many have competed in national and international tournaments.

Kabaddi *players*

Kabaddi is a popular sport among Sikhs, especially in rural areas. In *Kabaddi*, the players are divided into two teams and the field is divided into two parts with a line drawn down the middle.

A player from the team on the offense crosses the line while continuously reciting "*Kabaddi, Kabaddi, Kabaddi* . . ." The rest of the players on the offensive team are idle. All the players on the defensive team line up in a row, usually forming an arc, to try to corner the offensive player. The object of the offensive player is to touch any defensive player, run back, and touch the dividing line with any part of his body, without breaking the recitation of "*Kabaddi, Kabaddi.*" Once a defensive player has been touched, he can grab, hold, and wrestle the offensive player, and keep him on his side of the field and away from the dividing line, until he breaks the "*Kabaddi, Kabaddi*" recitation.

If the offensive player does not get back to touch the dividing line, a point is awarded to the defensive team. If the offensive player is successful in touching the dividing line, neither team gets the point.

The two teams take turns in sending the offensive players to the other side. When a set time period (usually one hour) has elapsed, the game is finished and the team with the most points wins.

There are several *Kabaddi* tournaments held in various cities across Canada, especially during spring and summer months. Toronto and Vancouver host the biggest tournaments. Recently, the Kabaddi Canada Cup has been held in Toronto, attracting teams from various countries such as Canada, the United States, the United Kingdom, India, and Pakistan. It attracts thousands of spectators and has large cash prizes for the winning team.

Sikh Culture and Traditions

Paul (Bubli) Chohan

Paul (Bubli) Chohan is a distinguished field hockey player. In the last seventeen years, he has represented Canada in three Olympics, three World Cups, two hundred international test matches, and many international tournaments. He holds the record number of competitions participated in by a Canadian field hockey player.

Born in Panjab, Chohan immigrated to Canada in 1964 at the age of six. He started playing field hockey at ten. Within four years he was on the Canadian National Junior Field Hockey team. When Chohan was sixteen, he was selected to play on the Canadian National Senior team. Today, he is still playing for them. He has traveled to more than fifty countries around the world.

Chohan lives in Vancouver with his wife and their two daughters.

Education

Khalsa School of Vancouver

The Khalsa School opened in Vancouver in 1986. There are at present 360 students enrolled in classes from preschool to Grade 10. The average class size is twenty-five. The school plans to expand to Grade 12 and to add residence facilities for students in the next few years.

Khalsa School of Vancouver.

At the Khalsa School, the school day is extended by one hour. The extra time is used to teach the students the Sikh religion and values. The school emphasizes the teaching of human values and tolerance. During this time, they are also taught the Panjabi language and Sikh *kirtan* and music classes are held. Khalsa School offers many extracurricular activities such as field trips, sports, and community projects. Students have taken part in many contests and have won several prizes.

The school receives 50 per cent of its funding from the B.C. Ministry of Education. The Satnam Education Society, which is the school's sponsoring body, donates 30 per cent, and the rest comes from tuition. The school is open to students of all religions and backgrounds, but is operated in conformance with the religious and secular traditions of Sikhism. More than half of the teachers are non-Sikhs. The British Columbia Ministry of Education has granted Class I independent status to the school, the highest category for such schools.

Dashmesh Punjabi School

Dashmesh Punjabi School is a private Sikh school located in Abbotsford, a suburb of Vancouver, B.C. It was founded in 1986 and currently offers classes to 180 students, from kindergarten to grade 7. The school covers the regular B.C. curriculum and the instruction day is extended to teach students the Panjabi language, Sikh history, *Gurbani Shabad Kirtan* (hymn singing), and Indian classical music.

The school has 14 teachers, about half of whom are non-Sikhs. The classes are held at the Khalsa Diwan Society Sikh Gurdwara in Abbotsford. Recently, the School Society has bought 20 acres of land in the area, with plans for a new secondary school building and to expand the school to grade 12.

Panjabi Language and Gurmukhi Script

A sample of Gurmuhki *script is shown on page 27 of this book.*

As stated earlier, Sikhs have their own spoken and written language. The *Gurmukhi* script has thirty-five letters in its alphabet and is a phonetically-based language, similar to English. It has some sounds which do not exist in English. It also has letters for some sounds for which two letters have to be combined in English, such as *sh* and *th*. It should be noted that Panjabi is also the mother tongue of Muslims in northern India and Pakistan; however, they use the Arabic script. Knowing the Panjabi language and *Gurmukhi* script is necessary for Sikhs to read and understand their culture and the Sikh holy scriptures.

Sikh Culture and Traditions

Sikh Organizations and the Sikh Press

There are more than two hundred Sikh cultural and religious organizations across Canada. They can be found in all major Canadian cities. These organizations serve the social and educational needs of the Sikh communities. They offer courses on the Panjabi language and music to children. They also act as charitable organizations. Some of these Sikh organizations produce and distribute books and cassette tapes on Sikh literature and religious music. The religious organizations in Toronto and Vancouver offer weekly religious programs on radio and television. Sikh co-operative credit unions have also been established in Vancouver and Toronto.

The Sikh cultural organizations in Canada offer classes on *Bhangra* and *Gidda* dances. Many people learn the folk dances through these organizations. They are also responsible for bringing weekly programs, such as Panjabi movies and plays, to local radio and television stations. These organizations have helped publish books, magazines, and newspapers on Sikh and Panjabi history and literature.

A collection of Sikh newspapers and magazines.

World Sikh Organization (WSO)

The World Sikh Organization (WSO) is a non-profit organization that represents members of the Sikh community on international and national issues. Its headquarters are in Washington, D.C., with offices and members around the world. The WSO's Canadian branch is very active, with an office in Ottawa.

Sikh Culture and Traditions

Macauliffe Institute of Sikh Studies

The Macauliffe Institute of Sikh Studies was founded in 1985. It was named after M.A. Macauliffe, who was a Sikh scholar living in Panjab in the last quarter of the nineteenth century. The purpose of this organization is to promote the study and research of the history, philosophy, and culture of the Sikhs. The Macauliffe Institute is headquartered in Toronto.

National Alliance of Canadian Sikhs (NACS)

The National Alliance of Canadian Sikhs was formed in 1992. Headquartered in Toronto, the Alliance strives to be the collective voice of the Sikhs in Canada, especially as it relates to the social services and services to the youth. It has branches in all regions of Canada and in all major Canadian cities.

International Sikh Youth Federation (ISYF)

Headquartered in Surrey, B.C., the International Sikh Youth Federation has branches in Toronto and major cities across Canada. They have several religious, social, and political functions. The ISYF has many members across the country and represents its members to federal and provincial governments across Canada. They put special emphasis on communicating the human rights concerns of the Sikhs living in India.

Chapter Four

SIKHS IN CANADA TODAY

*People of virtue eat the bread of their labour,
only the false and the deceitful live by begging.*
—Guru Ram Das, the Fourth Guru

Sikhs have been coming to Canada for nearly a century. During this time, they have struggled to overcome many social and economic hardships. Sikhs have been successful in establishing themselves in Canadian society. In this chapter you will read about some Sikh individuals, their contributions to Canada, and how Sikhs have very much become a part of today's Canada.

Charity

One of the teachings of Sikhism is to donate 10 per cent of one's income to charity and to help the needy. It is difficult to estimate the number of Sikhs who adhere to this directive, but many do give generously to charity. An outstanding example is Stephen Sander.

Stephen Sander

Stephen Sander was born in 1934 in Panjab, India. His original name was Sukhwant Singh Mehta. In India, he worked as an office clerk to help support his family and attended night school to become a teacher of physical education. Sukhwant came to Nova Scotia in 1960 and taught physical education there. He furthered his studies and eventually received a Master's degree in physical education. Sukhwant officially changed his name to Stephen Sander after graduation.

In 1963 Sander moved to British Columbia. He continued teaching for some time until he was dismissed from his teaching position. Sander had to sell his house so he could move to another town to work. He made a huge profit from the sale, and became very interested in real estate. He gave up teaching and began to invest heavily in real estate. He became very rich through his investments; by 1989, his investments were estimated at more than $110 million.

Sander worked in the real estate business until the late 1980s when he suddenly lost interest in it and became very interested in metaphysics and spirituality. He studied these in great depth. He also studied Sikhism and became knowledgeable about the religion.

On December 25, 1989, Sander announced the founding of the Consciousness International Foundation, an organization to serve people from all ethnic, racial, and religious backgrounds. The purpose of the organization is to help the sick and the poor of the world. After his announcement, Sander transferred ownership of 90 per cent of his real estate investments to the foundation. When asked why he did this, he explained, "I have made a lot of money. I did this for my soul, and I feel relieved and happy in sharing with the less fortunate."

Entrepreneurs

Many Sikhs in Canada today are entrepreneurs. Entrepreneurship is the fastest growing segment of Canadian business. Many Sikh Canadians go into entrepreneurship because they believe it has good possibilities for growth.

Most businesses owned by Sikh Canadians are jointly owned by members of the same family. This means two or more members of the same family, for example, two brothers and their families, put their money together to start a business and share the responsibilities of running it. The Kaur sisters' furniture business is one such example.

Fair Deal Furniture

Fair Deal Furniture began operations in 1985. It has a manufacturing facility in Toronto, as well as six retail stores in Toronto and two stores in Calgary. Three families, related through two sisters, Sarjeet and Sarindar, collectively own the business. They attribute the success of their business to the exceptional degree of trust and understanding among the family members. Strong religious beliefs also help in gaining trust and rapport with their customers.

Sikhs in Canada Today

Sarjeet Kaur in one of the Fair Deal stores she runs.

Lumber Industry

When the Sikhs first came to Canada in the early 1900s, many of them settled in British Columbia and worked in sawmills. Over the years, many of them have gone into the lumber business and became very successful, such as Harbans Singh Doman of Doman Industries Ltd.

Harbans Singh (Herb) Doman

Herb Doman's father came to Canada in 1906. He was one of the partners of the Mayo Lumber Company in Paldi, British Columbia. When Herb was twelve years old, his father died. Herb had to drop out of school and work to support the family. Eventually he, too, went into the lumber business. In 1955, he established Doman Industries Ltd. Today the company has nearly three thousand employees, making it one of the largest lumber companies in Canada. Herb Doman lives with his family in Duncan, British Columbia.

Banking

Banking is an important part of modern society. There are more than 100 000 people employed in the banking business in Canada. Among these are some Sikh Canadians who have been very successful in the banking world, such as Sarabjit Marwah.

Sarabjit (Sabi) S. Marwah
Sabi Marwah was born and raised in Calcutta, India. After receiving his doctorate in economics in India, he went to the United States to study business administration. In 1978, Sabi moved to Toronto armed with his MBA degree. Not long after he arrived in Toronto, he began to work for the Bank of Nova Scotia as a financial analyst. His career blossomed and he was promoted several times. In 1994, Sabi was appointed Executive Vice-president of the Bank of Nova Scotia. Marwah is one of the few turbaned Sikh Canadians who have been promoted to a very high level in a large Canadian corporation.

Transportation

Sikhs around the world have always been active in the transportation industries in disproportionate numbers. Many work as taxi, bus, and truck drivers. India, Singapore, Malaysia, and many other countries have large numbers of Sikhs working as airline and air force pilots. It will be interesting to see if Sikhs in Canada follow this path.

A willingness to work hard, desire for an independent life, and chance for reward are usually cited as the reason for this preference.

Farming

Although many of the Sikhs who came to Canada in the early 1900s were farmers in Panjab, many of them took jobs in British Columbia sawmills. It has only been in the last twenty years that Sikhs in any number have gone into farming. Today, there are about 10 000 Sikh Canadian farmers and farm workers. They have even formed a farm workers union on the West Coast. One of the biggest farms is owned by Gurdev Sandhu.

Sandhu Farms

Gurdev Singh Sandhu and his family came to Canada in 1966. Gurdev studied economics at Simon Fraser University for two years. In 1974, the Sandhu family purchased a farm in Abbotsford, British Columbia. The Sandhus worked very hard to expand their business and, today, theirs is one of the largest farms in the Fraser Valley. During peak seasons, they employ between six and seven hundred workers. Sandhus Farms produces fruits and vegetables and distributes its produce in British Columbia, Alberta, Manitoba, Ontario, Washington, and Idaho.

Sorting produce at Sandhu Farms.

Rajinder Kaur

Rajinder Kaur is a farm worker living in British Columbia. She came to Canada from Panjab, India, in 1985. She routinely puts in twelve-hour days at a local farm picking berries. Since coming to Canada, she has had to work very hard—a lot harder than she ever worked in India. As is typical of many immigrants, she sees her hard work as a necessary sacrifice to establish herself and her family in their new land.

Sikhs in Canada Today

Sports

One of the teachings of the Sikh Gurus was the importance of a healthy body. Sikhs practise this teaching through exercise and participation in different sports. Several Sikh Canadians have excelled in sports. Pamela Rai, the swimmer, won a bronze medal in the 1984 Los Angeles Olympic games and a gold medal in the 1986 Edinburgh Commonwealth games. Another athlete, Harpal Singh Talhan of Quesnel, B.C., was the Canadian lightweight boxing champion in 1990.

Dave Sidoo

Dave Sidoo was born in New Westminster in 1959. He was the first Sikh Canadian to become a professional athlete. Dave excelled in many sports, but decided to concentrate on football. He attended the University of British Columbia and played for the UBC Thunderbirds from 1978 to 1982. As a professional player for six years, he played for the Saskatchewan Roughriders and the British Columbia Lions in the Canadian Football League. Dave retired from professional football in 1988 and now works as a stockbroker. He and his wife, Manjit, live in Vancouver.

Robin Bawa

Robin Bawa is another outstanding Sikh Canadian athlete. His grandfather, Bawa Singh Johal, came to Canada in 1906. (Robin's father was one of those Sikhs who followed the trend of adopting his father's first name as a last name.) Robin was born in Duncan, British Columbia. He played junior hockey for the Kamloops Blazers. He was also selected to play on the Western Hockey League All Star Team. Robin has played with the Washington Capitals, Vancouver Canucks, San Jose Sharks, and Anaheim Mighty Ducks in the National Hockey League.

Tiger Jeet Singh

This forty-seven-year-old, 191 cm, 120 kg (6'3", 260 lbs) Sikh Canadian from Toronto is a living legend in Japan, especially in the wrestling world. Tiger Jeet Singh has won many national and international championships. Born in India, he moved to Canada in 1968 where he trained under an Australian coach, Fred Atkins, who named him Tiger in recognition of his strength and aggressiveness. During the 1970s, Tiger wrestled in Toronto, Australia, New Zealand, Fiji, and many other countries, before many sold out stadiums of up to 55 000 spectators. In 1972, he got his start in Japan and has never looked back. He is extremely popular throughout that country and travels there six times a year.

Tiger has his own line of clothing, dolls, comics, and many other items, all especially popular in Japan. Profiles on Tiger and his career have appeared in the media throughout the world, including CBC's "Fifth Estate."

Tiger works with civic leaders and police in the Toronto area to promote a drug free lifestyle among his followers, especially the youth. He is now training his son Tiger Junior, Gurjit Singh, to wrestle. Tiger Junior was recently given the wrestling rookie of the year award in Japan.

Tiger Jeet Singh and Tiger Junior (to his left) posing with staff in Tiger's sporting goods store, Malton, Ontario.

Sikhs in Canada Today

Politics

Sikhs have been active in Canadian politics for more than thirty-five years. In 1956, Niranjan Singh Garewal became the first Sikh Canadian to run for election to a Canadian legislature. Dr. Gulzar Cheema has been elected to the Manitoba legislature. British Columbia has three Sikh Canadian NDP MLAs, Harry Lally, Ujjal Dasanjh, and Moe Sihota. Alberta has elected a Sikh Progressive Conservative MLA, Harry Sohal from Calgary. Sikhs participate in all three major political parties in Canada.

In the 1993 federal election, two Sikhs were elected as Members of Parliament—Harbans Singh (Herb) Dhaliwal from Vancouver, B.C. and Gurbax Singh Malhi from Malton, Ontario.

Manmohan Singh (Moe) Sihota
In 1986, Moe Sihota became the first Sikh Canadian elected to be an MLA. In 1991, he was appointed British Columbia's Minister of Labour and Consumer Services and Minister Responsible for Constitutional Affairs.

Gurbax Singh Malhi
Gurbax Singh Malhi was the first turbaned Sikh to be elected to the Canadian Parliament. He represented the riding of Malton, near Toronto.

Professionals

As you have read in Chapter One, most of the Sikhs who came to Canada with the second wave of immigration were better educated than their predecessors; many were professionals.

Wallace T. Oppal

Born in Duncan, British Columbia, Mr. Justice Wallace T. Oppal was the first Sikh Canadian to be appointed to the Supreme Court of British Columbia. His father died when he was nine and his mother was left to raise him and his brother. Oppal received his law degree from the University of British Columbia in 1966. Before his appointment to the Supreme Court of British Columbia, Oppal was a prominent criminal lawyer and crown prosecutor.

Oppal is a firm believer in Sikhism. He is in favour of the RCMP's decision to allow Sikhs to wear turbans as part of their uniform. He also believes minorities should be well-represented in the RCMP and other law-enforcing institutions.

Baltej Singh Dhillon

Born and raised in Malaysia, Baltej Singh Dhillon came to Canada in 1983. After finishing high school, he studied criminology at the University of British Columbia. He worked as a volunteer for the neighbourhood crime prevention program.

In 1985, Baltej decided to join the RCMP but, at that time, the RCMP did not allow Sikhs to wear turbans as part of their uniform. Baltej was forced to postpone his ambition because as a Sikh he was required by his religion to wear a turban. In the meantime, the RCMP commissioner recommended to the Solicitor General that the Sikhs in the RCMP be allowed to wear articles that are required by their religion. The recommendation was approved on March 15, 1990. The approval made it possible for Baltej to pursue his career with the RCMP. He became the first Sikh RCMP to wear a turban.

Sikhs in Canada Today

Baltej Dhillon in RCMP uniform and turban.

Recently, Baltej received praise and recognition for his work in solving a longstanding case that involved four Quesnel, British Columbia physicians who forged signatures to claim medical insurance benefits.

Entertainment

Monika Deol

Born in Panjab and raised in Manitoba, Monika Deol now lives in Toronto where she works in the television entertainment industry. She hosts three television programmes, co-hosts "The Fax" show (broadcast across Canada by MuchMusic), and is an anchor/reporter for the entertainment section of the evening news on CITY-TV.

"I am very proud of my Sikh heritage," she says. "My parents have always stressed the importance of Sikh teachings. There has always been a *Guru Granth Sahib* at home."

Art and Literature

The tradition of Sikh art and literature began with the Ten Gurus, several of whom were scholars and poets themselves and encouraged their followers to explore those areas. Sikhs have contributed to the world of art and literature. Sikh writers write in Panjabi and English; there are more than forty Sikh Canadian writers of Panjabi literature who have written novels, poems, plays, and travelogues. Many of their works have been published and sold in India, Canada, and other countries.

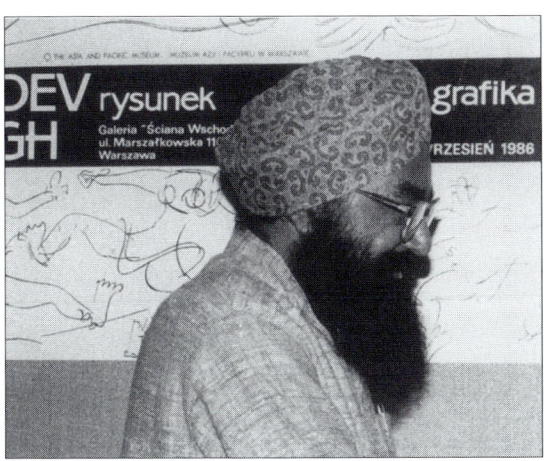

Hardev Singh

Hardev Singh is a worldfamous painter and artist. Born and raised in Panjab, he studied art at the Art College in Delhi. After graduation, he returned to Panjab for a short time, then joined the National Gallery of Modern Art in New Delhi.

Hardev went to Italy for three years on a fellowship offered by the Italian government. He traveled around the country and painted extensively. His works were exhibited in Rome. Shortly after his return to Panjab from Italy, Hardev went to Poland on a fellowship awarded by the Ministry of Art and Culture. Hardev lived in Poland for three years. While there, he met and married his wife, who is an art historian.

Hardev came to Canada in 1968. He became the regional director of art galleries in Ontario. For the last twenty years, Hardev has been working as a freelance artist. He has made a short film and has published four books on modern art and collections of his poems, paintings, sketches, and lithographs. One of his books, *Folk Tales and Proverbs of Punjab*, has been translated into Polish, German, Norwegian, Panjabi, and Italian.

Hardev's work is on display in national galleries in over thirty countries around the world.

Sarindar Dhaliwal

Sarindar is a thirty-nine-year-old artist living in Kingston, Ontario. Born in India, she was raised in England and studied art in both England and Canada. Her paintings combine fragments from her past such as photographs and mementos, with favourite organic plants, such as flowers, trees, foliage, and fruits arranged geometrically. She has also written short stories. Her work has appeared in exhibitions throughout Canada and has received very positive reviews.

Dayal Kaur Khalsa

Dayal Kaur Khalsa was born in New York City in 1943. She later moved to Montreal. Dayal adopted the Sikh religion in 1980. She wrote seven children's books, some of which have won awards in Canada and the United States. Dayal wrote about ordinary childhood experiences which she turned into interesting celebrations of the family. Tragically, Dayal died in 1989 at the age of forty-six.

 CONCLUSION

Sikhs have been making Canada their home for the last one hundred years. Today, there are approximately 240 000 Sikh Canadians, with Toronto and Vancouver having the largest Sikh populations.

Despite their relatively small population, Sikh Canadians have managed to retain their distinct culture, language, religion, and heritage. At the same time, they have adapted quite successfully to their new country. There are more than 80 Sikh *Gurdwaras* in Canada, and Sikh and Panjabi books, newspapers, magazines, TV and radio shows, sports tournaments, and cultural events are becoming more common every day.

Up until the 1970s, Sikhs faced severe challenges and discrimination in Canada. Over the last 20 years, most of these barriers have come down, and Sikhs now participate in every facet of Canadian life. At the same time, there has been serious political turmoil in India. These factors, coupled with the fact that one-third to one-half of Sikh Canadians were born in Canada, make them very proud to be Canadian.

Trends of the last two decades indicate that Sikhs should have a bright future in the Canadian multicultural mosaic. This is part of what makes Canada a great country with a wonderful future!

Glossary

Achkan:	a coat
Akhand Path:	continuous reading of the *Guru Granth Sahib* from cover to over, taking forty-eight hours
Amrit:	initiation
Amrit:	"nectar of immortality," used in initiation ceremonies
Anand Karaj:	the religious part of a Sikh wedding, or "The Ceremony of Bliss"
Baisakhi:	the most important Sikh festival, usually held on April 13, on the day the Tenth Guru established the order of the Khalsa
Barat:	groom's wedding party
Bhangra:	a traditional Sikh folk dance
Bindi:	the red spot that Sikh women put on their foreheads to beautify themselves
Chunni:	a long scarf used by women and made of fine, lightweight materials
Dastar:	a turban, worn to cover a Sikh's uncut hair
Diwali:	a festival of lights celebrated throughout the Indian subcontinent
Gidda:	a traditional Sikh folk dance for women
Gurdwara:	a Sikh place of worship, or temple
Gurmukhi:	the script for the Panjabi language
Guru:	a holy man or a spiritual teacher; one who dispels ignorance or darkness (gu) and proclaims enlightenment (ru); one of the ten Sikh Gurus
Guru Granth Sahib:	the Sikh holy book or scriptures
Jhanjran:	a silver bracelet worn around the ankle
Kabaddi:	a popular rural sport from Panjab
Kacha:	short breeches, one of the Five Ks
Kanga:	a wooden comb, worn to represent a clean mind and body, one of the Five Ks

Glossary

Kara:	a steel bracelet worn on the wrist as a sign of the eternity of God, one of the Five Ks
Karah Parsad:	a sacrament made from purified butter, water, flour, and sugar
Kaur:	a Sikh middle or last name meaning "lioness or princess"
Kesadharis:	"ones with long hair," those who do not cut their hair, do wear turbans, but may or may not keep the other K's
Kes:	"uncut hair," represents a simple life, saintliness, wisdom, and devotion to God, one of the Five Ks
Khalsa:	the Sikh brotherhood, symbolized by the Five Ks, the kirpan, kes, kara, kanga, and kacha
Khanda:	the symbol of Sikhism
Kirpan:	a sword worn by Sikhs, representing freedom and indomitable spirit, one of the Five Ks
Kirtan:	hymns sung and recited at Sikh congregations accompanied with music
Kurta:	a style of shirt
Langar:	means "free kitchen" in a *Gurdwara* or a Sikh congregation, run voluntarily with free serving of food
Maharaja:	"great king "
Milni:	a ceremony of union of the two families at a wedding
Misls:	militias
Pakoras:	a favourite Sikh snack
Palla:	a piece of long cloth used at Sikh weddings to symbolize union
Panj Pyares:	the "five beloved ones"
Panjab:	"the land of five rivers," Panjab is one of the states of India and a place of origin for many Sikhs
Paranda:	a decoration braided into the hair
Patkas:	head coverings worn by Sikh boys before they start wearing turbans at adolescence

Glossary

Purdah:	a veil usually worn by women and one of the customs Sikh Gurus tried to abolish
Raagis:	professional religious singers
Rakhri:	"ribbon," a festival that celebrates the love between brothers and sisters in which the sister ties a ribbon around her brother's wrist and he gives her the gift of money
Roti:	an unleavened bread made from whole wheat flour
Sahajdharis:	"slow adapters," those who observe only some Sikh teachings and requirements
Salwaar-kameez:	traditional apparel for Sikh women, also called a Panjabi suit
Sangeet:	a wedding shower
Sati:	burning of widows on their husbands' funeral pyres, a practice disapproved of by Sikhs
Shabad Kirtan:	singing of hymns
Sikh:	"disciple," a follower of the Sikh religion
Singh:	a Sikh middle or last name, meaning "lion"
Tamba:	a sash worn at the waist with a kurta-style shirt

Sikh Gurdwaras in Canada

Alberta

1. Sikh Society, Old Banff Coach Road and 81 St. SW, Calgary

2. Sikh Youth Federation of Canada, 135 Martindale Blvd., NE, Calgary

3. Nanaksar Gurdwara Gursikh Temple, 1410 Horse Hills Road, RR 6, Edmonton

4. Sikh Society of Alberta, 14211 - 133 Ave., Edmonton

5. Sri Guru Singh Sabha Society, 9750 - 47 Ave., Edmonton

6. Ramgarhia Sikh Society, 2606 Millwoods Rd. East, Edmonton

7. Fort McMurray Sikh Society, 174 McConachie Cres., Fort McMurray

8. Gursikh Missionary Society Temple, Grande Prairie

British Columbia

9. Khalsa Diwan Society, 33089 South Fraser Way, Abbotsford

10. Canadian Ramgarhia Society, 6908 MacPherson Ave., Burnaby

11. Guru Teg Bahadur, Sikh Temple Society, P.O. Box 298, Clearwater

12. Vancouver Island Sikh Cultural Society, 3210 Sherman Rd., Duncan

13. Gursikh Temple, P.O. Box 1719, Fort St. James

14. Golden Sikh Temple, South 13th St., Golden

15. Sikh Society, Comp 7, Site 8-S.S.1, Houston

16. Sikh Cultural Society, 700 Cambridge St., Kamloops

17. Okanagan Sikh Temple and Cultural Society, 1101 North Rutland Rd., Kelowna

18. Kitimat Sikh Society, 1600 Nalabila St., Kitimat

19. Khalsa Diwan Society, P.O. Box 684, Lake Cowichan

Sikh Gurdwaras in Canada

20. Mackenzie Sikh Society, P.O. Box 2407, Mackenzie

21. Merritt Sikh Society, 2190 Granite Ave., P.O. Box 1552, Merritt

22. Mission Gursikh Society, 33193 - 7th Ave., Mission

23. Vancouver Island Khalsa Diwan Society, 328-3rd St., Nanaimo

24. Paldi Khalsa Diwan Society, Paldi (near Duncan)

25. Penticton Sikh Temple, 3290 South Main St., Penticton

26. Khalsa Diwan Society, 347 Wood St., New Westminster

27. Sikh Temple, P.O. Box 833, 100 Mile House

28. Guru Gobind Singh Sikh Temple, 443 Kelly St. S., Prince George

29. Sikh Association Temple, 200 - 4th Ave. East, Prince Rupert

30. Prince Rupert Sikh Missionary Society, 1945 McNicholl St., Prince Rupert

31. Alberni Valley Gurdwara Society, 4741 Montrose, Port Alberni

32. Khalsa Diwan Society, 3558 - 12th Ave., Port Alberni

33. Guru Arjan Dev Sikh Society, P.O. Box 213, Powell River

34. Cariboo Gur Sikh Temple Society, 431 Lewis Dr., Quesnel

35. India Cultural Centre of Canada Gurdwara, 8600, Number 5 Road, Richmond

36. Nanak Sar Gursikh Temple, 18691 Westminster Hwy., Richmond

37. Squamish Sikh Society, 37947 - 5th Ave., Squamish

38. Guru Nanak Sikh Temple, 7050 - 120th St., Surrey

39. Skeena Valley Guru Nanak Temple, P.O. Box 245, Terrace

40. Akali Singh Sikh Society, 1890 Skeena St., Vancouver

41. Khalsa Diwan Society, 8000 Ross St., Vancouver

42. North Okanagan Sikh Cultural Society, 3800 Common Age Cres., Vernon

43. Khalsa Diwan Society, 1210 Topaz Ave., Victoria

44. Punjabi Akali Singh Society, 2721 Graham St., Victoria

45. Guru Nanak Temple Society, 3024 Glendale Dr., Williams Lake

46. Western Sikh Sabha, 974 Houston St., Williams Lake

Sikh Gurdwaras in Canada

Manitoba

47. Sikh Society of Western Manitoba, 3704 Van Horne Ave., Brandon
48. Sikh Society of Thompson, P.O. Box 973, Thompson
49. Sikh Society of Manitoba, 1244 Mollard Rd., Winnipeg
50. Singh Sabha of Winnipeg, 11 Sturgeon Place, Winnipeg
51. Khalsa Diwan Society, 807 Macleod, Winnipeg
52. Sikh Center, 500 Dover Court, Winnipeg
53. Gurdwara Nanaksar, 255 St. David Rd., Winnipeg

Newfoundland

54. Newfoundland Sikh Society, 47 Ruteledge Cres., St. John's

Nova Scotia

55. Maritime Sikh Society, 10 Parkhill Rd., Halifax
56. Glace Bay Sikh Society, 9 Khalsa Dr., Glace Bay

Ontario

57. Golden Triangle Sikh Association Temple, Baden (near Kitchener-Waterloo)
58. Nanaksar Satsang Sabha, 64 Timberland Dr., Brampton
59. Sikh Association of Brantford, P.O. Box 1802, Brantford
60. Guru Ravidas Sabha, 2266 Queensway Dr., Burlington
61. Siri Guru Singh Sabha, RR #2, N. Dumfries, Cambridge
62. Guelph Sikh Society, P.O. Box 150, Guelph

Sikh Gurdwaras in Canada

63. Gurdwara Sikh Sangat, 200 Old Guelph Rd., Hamilton

64. Ramgarhia Gurdwara, Lake Avenue North, Hamilton

65. Kingston Sikh Cultural Association, 823 Slocan Place, Kingston

66. London Sikh Society Temple, 37 Clark Rd., London

67. Sri Guru Singh Sabha Gurdwara, 7282 Airport Rd., Malton

68. Sikh Sangat of Canada, Suite 225, 7305 Woodbine Ave., Markham

69. Ontario Khalsa Darbar, 7080 Dixie Rd., Mississauga

70. Ramgarhia Association of Ontario, 1623 Cormack Cres., Mississauga

71. Sikh Missionary Society, 7286 Sills Rd., Mississauga

72. Ottawa Sikh Society, 25 Gurdwara Rd., Nepean

73. Ramgarhia Sikh Society of Toronto, 140 Rivalda Rd., North York

74. Oakville Sikh Cultural Association, 1361 Rebecca St., Oakville

75. Gursikh Sabha Canada, 905 Middlefield Rd., Scarborough

76. Guru Ram Das Ashram, 348 Palmerston Blvd., Toronto

77. Shromani Sikh Society, 269 Pape Ave., Toronto

78. Siri Guru Singh Sabha, 331 Old Weston Rd., Toronto

79. Sikh Cultural Society of Metro Windsor, 5225 Howard Rd., Windsor

Quebec

80. Gurdwara Sahib Quebec, 2183 Wellingon St., Montreal

81. Sikh Temple Association, 1090 St. Joseph Street, Lachine

Saskatchewan

82. Sikh Society of Regina, 639 Pasqua St., Regina

83. Sikh Society of Saskatoon, 312 Avenue 1 South, Saskatoon

SIKH CALENDAR

Sikh religious and social festivals follow the lunar based Sikh calendar. Lunar calendars are based on movements of the moon around the earth, whereas solar calendars are based on movements of earth around the sun. Festivals based on the Sikh calendar fall on different days each year on the solar calendar.

For example, in the solar calendar that Canadians use, the New Year begins on the first day of the first month, January. In the Sikh lunar calendar, the New Year begins on the first day of the second month, Baisakh. Therefore, the Sikh New Year falls on April 13 or 14.

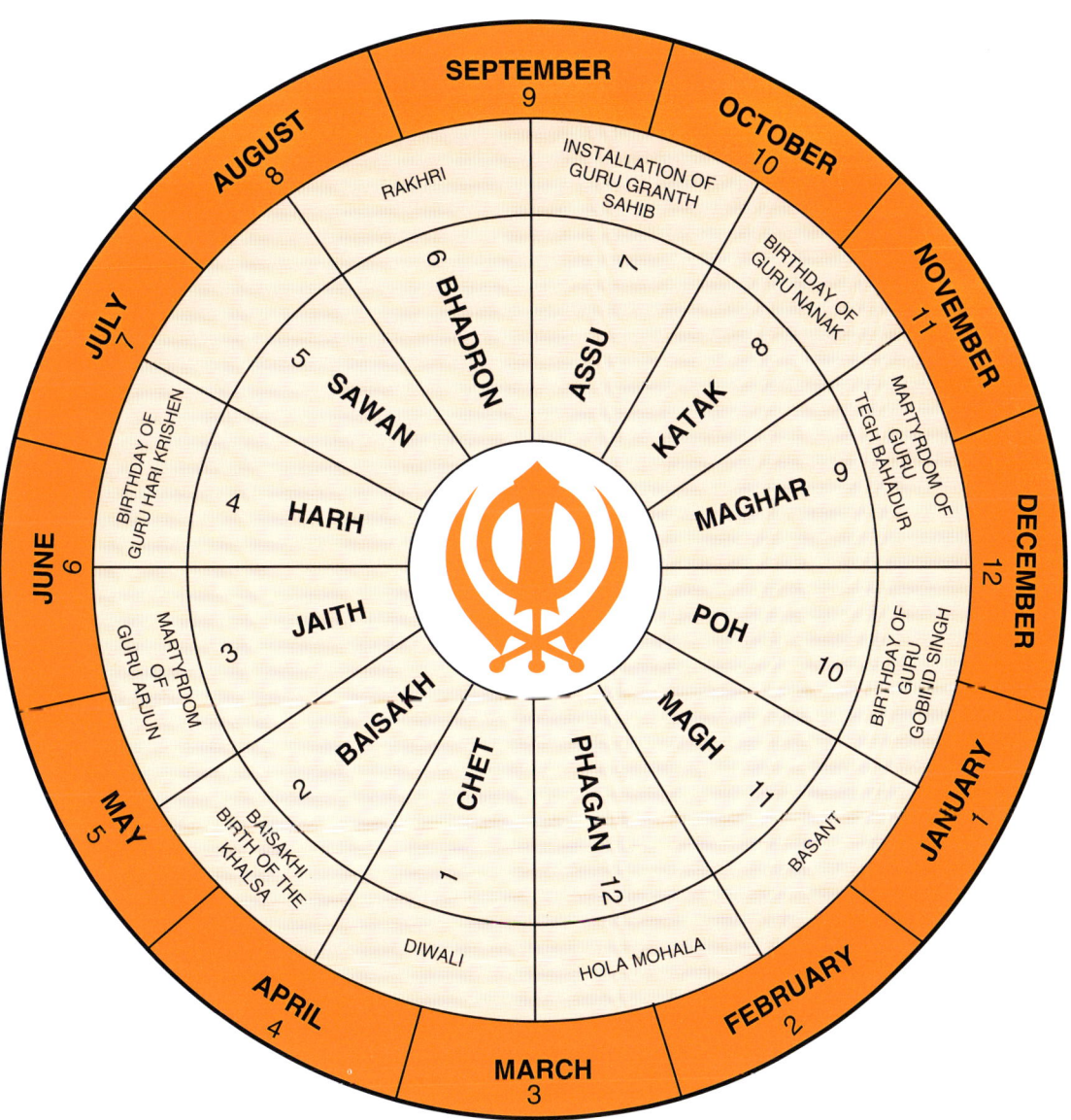

Suggested Reading List

Buchignani, Norman and Indra, Doreen. *Continuous Journey: A Social History of South Asians in Canada.* Toronto: McClelland & Stewart Limited, 1985.

Cole, W. Owen and Sambhi, Piara Singh. *The Sikhs: Their Religious Beliefs and Practices.* New Delhi: Vikas Publishing House Pub. Ltd., 1978.

Ferguson, Ted. *A White Man's Country: An Exercise in Canadian Prejudice.* Toronto: Macmillan, 1975.

Gandhi, Surjit Singh. *History of the Sikh Gurus: A Comprehensive Study.* Jullundur: Gur Das Kapur & Sons (P) Ltd., 1978.

Gundara, Jaswinder. *Splintered Dreams: Sikhs in Southern Alberta.* Calgary: Arusha International Development Resource Centre, 1985.

Johnston, Hugh. *The Voyage of the Komagata Maru: The Sikh Challenge to Canada's Colour Bar.* Delhi: Oxford University Press, 1979.

Muthana, I.M. *People of India in North America.* Vancouver: Author, 1982.

O'Connell, Joseph, Israel, Milton, and Oxtoby, Willard. *Sikh History and Religion in the Twentieth Century.* Toronto: University of Toronto Press, 1988.

Singh, Harbans. *The Heritage of the Sikhs.* Columbia: South Asia Books, 1983.

Singh, Kesar. *Canadian Sikhs.* Surrey, B.C.: Author, 1989.

Singh, Khushwant. *A History of the Sikhs.* 2 Vols. Princeton: Princeton Univ. Press, 1966.

Singh, Parkash. *The Sikh Gurus and the Temple of Bread.* Amritsar: Shiromani Gurdwara Parbandhak Committee, 1971.